SUGAR AND SPICE & TRIAL RUN

This double volume of plays by the author of *Class Enemy* is published alongside the first production of *Sugar and Spice* at the Royal Court Theatre, London in September 1980. As in *Class Enemy,* for which Williams was jointly named the year's most promising playwright, the protagonists in *Sugar and Spice* are teenage kids. *Sugar and Spice,* however, is a departure for Williams, being essentially a savagely realistic love story – set in a tatty council flat off the King's Road, Chelsea.

The second play, *Trial Run,* first presented by the Oxford Playhouse Company in Oxford, London and on tour, is a sharp political fable about a siege in the basement of the Hounslow Woolworth's. The hostages are white, their captors black, but the motives turn out to be very mixed indeed.

SUGAR AND SPICE
&
TRIAL RUN

Two Plays by

NIGEL WILLIAMS

A Methuen New Theatrescript
Eyre Methuen · London

For Suzan, Ned and Jack

First published in Great Britain in 1980 by Eyre Methuen Ltd,
11 New Fetter Lane, London EC4P 4EE
Copyright © 1980 by Nigel Williams
Printed in Great Britain by Expression Printers Ltd, London

ISBN 0 413 46620 5

CAUTION

SUGAR AND SPICE

Sugar and spice and all things nice
That's what little girls are made of.
Rats and snails and puppy-dogs' tails
That's what little boys are made of.

Children's rhyme

Sugar and Spice was presented at the Royal Court Theatre, London on 9 October 1980 with the following cast:

SUZE	Carole Hayman
SHARON	Toyah Willcox
CAROL	Gwyneth Strong
TRACY	Tammi Jacobs
LINDA	Caroline Quentin
DEREK	John Fowler
STEVE	Daniel Peacock
LEROY	Leroi Samuels
JOHN	Tony London

Directed by Bill Alexander
Designed by Mary Moore
Lighting by Jack Raby

The action of the play takes place in SUZE's council flat off the King's Road.

Act One

Either side of the audience, from the back, come a group of girls and a boy. The boy, whose name is DEREK, should be as young or small or both as is convenient, and one of the girls of his age or size or both. Her name is LINDA and she has fair hair and the aspect of a tough, if undersized, milkmaid. She is eating chips, some, if not all of which, she offers to DEREK. The other three girls, TRACY, CAROL and SHARON, range in age from fifteen to seventeen, although their mixture of styles – the communal assurance of a group of schoolchildren combined with the edgy beginnings of adulthood, make it difficult to be too precise about their exact status in the world. TRACY is a hard-faced camp-follower with a terrifyingly low boredom threshold, CAROL is a very pretty, dark, nervous girl, who, for the best part of the action of the play is popping pills of one kind or another, and SHARON at first sight has the look of a Russian tractor driver (female of course) – or a farm girl. Plain, thickset, very aggressive, she is naturally dominant without having anything of the parody lesbian about her manner. It is simply that the gestures that come most naturally to her are the ones the world usually describes as 'masculine'. All of the girls are more or less drunk. They are singing and waving Chelsea scarves. Their song goes –

'Air like wire an' teef like pearls,
We are
Ver Chelsea girls!
Dynamite rollers up our curls
We are
Ver Chelsea girls
1-2-3-4-
SLOANE SQUARE WANKERS!!!

At the climax of the song, up on the stage, where sits a tatty but exuberant council flat. Lots of booze and electrical gear, stereo etc. paintwork etc. in bad nick, but with a certain splendid style to it – through the doors at the back bursts SUZE. SUZE is a woman, somewhere between thirty and fifty, dressed with rather splendid inappropriateness, in punk gear. She looks like a cross between a bus conductress and an over the hill receptionist, but this does not hide her compulsive, all-embracing sexuality. SUZE has GOT to seduce everyone, and to accomplish this she uses a stunning repertoire of pouts, strokes and wiggles. With these girls she is more natural than with men. For the most part tonight she is speaking the way her mother did, and enjoying it. She is the drunkest of the lot.

SUZE: CARM ON UP GELS! SUZE'S IS ACH YORE DISPOSAL!

And up on the stage they climb, into this crowded flat, the walls of which are plastered with black and white pictures of women. Photographs. Or rather woman, for closer inspection would reveal that the woman, photographed hundreds of different times in hundreds of different poses, is none other than SUZE. And taking pride of place – three large wedding pictures in each of which is a different man. Around each wedding picture – pictures of the kids.

TRACY: You was dead right abaht ver lift.

SUZE: Woun' 'e lech yer in?

TRACY: Nah 'e fuckin' wouldn't.

SHARON: Too fuckin' common fer 'im.

LINDA: Ooo innit a lovely place you got Suze?

SUZE: Din't I say so.

SHARON: Vat fuckin' git in ve 'all.

CAROL: It was Derek. 'E reckoned Derek was out ter make chrouble.

DEREK: Leave off woncher?

ALL THE GIRLS: A-A-H!

DEREK: I never wan' ed ter come anyway.

CAROL: Don' be so fuckin' rude Derek. When someone arsts you back ter veir flat on such short acquaintance you might 'ave ver fuckin' grace ter cease fuckin' moanin' fer two minutes tergevver!

SUZE: Oh 'e's on'y a lit'l boy incher? Nah. Wot was we jrinkin'.

SHARON: We 'ad wine in vat pub. Till vey slung us aht. An' 'en we bought vat bottle a' . . .

SUZE: Whiskey. Thass the stuff. Everyone 'ave a lit'l whiskey will they?

CAROL: Ta.

TRACY: Fanks.

SHARON: Nice.

LINDA: Not fer me Suze. I don't. Oooh innit lovely though. 'Ow long you 'ad it?

SUZE: Iss a council flat in fact. An' I work from 'ome. When I work.

SHARON: Oh yeh?

SUZE: Yeh.

Unnerved by SHARON's stare she goes to the well-stocked drinks cupboard.

Well ainch yoo glad I plucked you off of ver schreet gels eh?

TRACY: Schreet's O.K.

SUZE: Young gels like you jrinkin' whiskey out of a bottle outside a' fuckin' Sainsbury's at 'alf past ten at night. Blimey. Anuvver ten minutes an' some copper'd a' done you under ver good ol' schreet offences act.

SHARON: Woss 'at then Suze?

SUZE: It is all abaht what is commonly known as prostitution innit?

SHARON: Geddaway.

SUZE: Ainch yoo rude?

But the veiled reference only brings her out in a pout and a leer. The attempt to seduce SHARON however won't wash. SHARON isn't a collaborator.

I was never like vis when I was a gel when between you an' me you could get pregnant jus' walkin' dahn ver fuckin' schreet an' lookin' in fuckin' shop winders.

SHARON: I bech yoo was a real tearawy Suze. Thass ver whiskey innit?

TRACY: I bet she was. I bet she was a right fuckin' raver.

SHARON: Was you invoved wig 'unjreds a' men Suze?

DEREK: Leave off woncher?

SHARON: All tergevver girls. An' this time Carol you can join in eh?

ALL: 'Air like wire an' teef like pearls
    We are
    Ver Chelsea girls
    Dynamite rollers up our curls
    We are ver
    Chelsea girls
    1 – 2 – 3 – 4
    SLOANE SQUARE WANKERS!!!

SUZE is handing round drinks. SHARON becomes rather charming and adult with a stiff whiskey in her hand.

SHARON: Seriously though Suze. Woch yoo do fer a livin'?

SUZE: Er . . . model.

SHARON: Oh yeah?

SUZE: No I am. Reely am.

CAROL (*keen*): Mus' be inchrestin' that?

SUZE: Oh it is. I mean it's very glamorous. You know?

SHARON: I got a fairly good idea Suze.

TRACY: Woch yoo model then Suze?

SUZE: Cloves. You know. Gear an' 'at.

She poses, half satirical, half unintentionally ludicrous.

Punk. Noo wave.

TRACY: Fuckin' 'ell.

SUZE: Wot I am wearin' is wot I model. I mean I model wot I wear. So I'm never caught lookin' shabby know wot I mean? Twenny-four hours a day I am . . . smart.

CAROL: Yore in ver place fer vat though aincher Suze? I mean Chelsea is ver place fer that innit? Modellin'. I mean iss bung full a' models innit? Eh?

SHARON: Don' get no models in Brixton Suze. Not real ones. Jus' ve ovver kind.

CAROL: Knock twice an' walk up.

SHARON: We never close. Nudge nudge. Know wot I mean?

The girls guffaw. After a fractional pause so does SUZE. She then recovers her equilibrium by vamping the air in front of her and taking a large drink.

DEREK: We're all Chelsea supporters. Fuck all ve ovvers. Fuck 'em rigid. Fuck 'em up veir arses I say. Fuck 'em.

Pause.

LINDA: Yore showin' yoreself up Derek.

DEREK: Me an' the gels. We are. We're Chelsea supporters. We're fuckin' Chelsea supporters.

All the girls, including, for once, LINDA, ignore him. TRACY who has been casing the joint fairly seriously returns to CAROL and SUZE.

TRACY: An' yoo got all them pitchers on ver wall an' all. 'Ow joo get inter modellin' Suze?

SUZE: I was spotted.

TRACY: No. Reely?

SUZE: Yeh. I was a dancer see. An' I was spotted.

CAROL: 'Ow joo get spotted then Suze?

SUZE *vamps till ready. All guffaw.*

SHARON: Ohh. Ainch yoo lovely?

CAROL: That P.V.C?

SUZE: It's a laminate plastic.

CAROL: Oh yeh.

CAROL: Does it crease?

SUZE: I wouldn't know love.

SHARON: She works in a jry cleaners. Thass why she's inchrested. Cloves is 'er main inchrest. Cloves an' woch she puts on 'er face an' fuckin boys. 'Er muvver's the fuckin' same. She loves 'er muvver.

CAROL: Like I love Rod Stewart I love 'er.

SUZE: You like Rod Stewart do you love?

SHARON: We 'ate Rod Stewart. We reckon 'e's schoopid.

SUZE: Oh *no!*

SHARON: We're reely dahn on 'im. Ain't we Trace? 'E looks like 'e's got some terrible disease a' the bowel when 'e's singin'. An' 'is 'air. Oh Gawd 'is 'air. Poofy lit'l 'airdo 'e's got 'en 'e? I mean if we wanna say sunnink's ve absolute bleed'n end we say you like it like you like Rod Stewart. Get it?

SUZE: So you 'ate yore Mum do yer Carol?

CAROL is very tense.

CAROL: Leave off Sharon eh?

SHARON: She got problems.

CAROL: LEAVE OFF!

TRACY: Linda an' Carol is soft in ve 'ead an' Linda an' Carol is soft in ve 'ead. Linda an' Carol is –

CAROL: Linda an' Carol wot eh? Wot?

TRACY: You know wot.

CAROL: Oh do I though?

TRACY: Oh you do. *You* do.

CAROL: Do I eh?

TRACY: Yes you fuckin' well –

SHARON: Leave it aht gels cancher?

Leave off a' Carol. We ain't gonna talk abaht Carol no more.

To SUZE. *Very much grown-up to grown-up.*

Carol's why we was on vat pavement. Carol's why we're up Chelsea. That an' Derek wan'ed ter see ver ground. On account 'e's a supporter. But Carol's why we're up Chelsea incher Carol. She likes ver posh life she does. An' she likes a boy ter look at doncher Carol. Well –

CAROL: I fought we wasn't goin' ter discuss me Sharon. Do you live here alone Suze?

SHARON: 'Ark at 'er. 'Do you live heah alone Suze?' Woch yoo wanna be Carol – receptionist or sunnink?

CAROL: Well woch yoo wanna be Sharon, Security Guard?

SHARON: I'm a Girl Mugger. I'm one a' them Girl Muggers you read abaht in ver Daily Mail. I 'ide be'ind bushes an' I leap aht at men an' I clobber 'em. An' 'en I ask 'em ter take me 'ome.

All the girls like this except CAROL *who has wandered, extra nervously, over towards the window.*

She's over the fuckin' winder nah in't she? Lookin' for 'em.

TRACY: These boys was follerin' us see Suze, and she reckoned one of 'em was follerin' 'er see? 'Cos ve uvver two was all shoutin' an' swearin' an' carryin' on but 'e was – yoo know – (*'Swoony' pose.*) Jus' lookin'.

CAROL: SHUCH YORE FACE!

SUZE: Oh you keep close ter vat winder then lovey. You keep close ter vat winder if yore lookin' out fer a boy. Boys is worf' it. I mean I've 'ad experience. I've 'ad so much fuckin' experience iss incredible reely that I'm still walkin' arahnd wivout me legs in plaster an' over ver years I come to the conclusion that, in gen'ral, boys is worf it. They get all over yer an' they mess yer abaht an' they wave their wosser-names ach yer. Blimey iss like ver Royal Tournament. But in the end, they're well worf it.

CAROL (*bored pose*): 'S rainin' again.

SUZE: Yeh well it does don' it from time ter time. All right lovey all right you watch from vere. You can see ve 'ole a' Chelsea, Kensington ver lot you can. If you look reely 'ard you can see Princess Margaret.

SHARON: She's the one wot lights up every two minutes.

SUZE: I see a lot a' them in fact.

SHARON: Yeah?

SUZE: Royals. I do in fact. I mean at parties an' suchlike. 'Eard 'a them. I mean not ter look at but I 'eard 'a them and wot they do. Across crowded rooms Viscount Linley. I 'eard abaht 'im. Pissed as a fart an' 'e was on'y eight. They're terrible jrinkers are ver Royals. Under the fuckin' table every night out a' their everlovin' skulls. Apparently.

SHARON: 'E ain't comin' yore friend Carol. 'E turned off wiv 'is mates. They gone over Albert Bridge, over ver fuckin' river back ter Wansworf where they belong. They don' allow juvenile delinquents in fuckin' Chelsea arter nine o'clock ?t night.

SUZE: Oh it is very pricey is Chelsea. Even council ain't cheap.

CAROL: 'E's ahtside. Vey're all ahtside.

A lift in tension. SHARON looks at SUZE. All of the others, apart from DEREK, who is staring gloomily at the carpet, and LINDA, who has taken over TRACY's voyage of exploration, though in a more ladylike fashion, case each other's reaction.

SHARON: Well well well.

CAROL: 'E's lookin' up 'ere. Ve uvvers ain't.

SHARON: Well well. Maybe 'e 'as fallen in love. Maybe 'e 'as decided that 'e mus' declare 'imself. 'E cannot lie. 'E 'as fallen in love wiv Derek.

DEREK: Fuck off.

She has joined CAROL at the window. Peers out.

SHARON: Iss 'im all right.

SUZE: Ask 'im up lovey. Ask yore friend up.

SHARON: You desperate an all?

SUZE: Maybe I am. It ain't none a' yore bleed'n business is it gel? These yore premises?

SHARON: No offence no offence.

LINDA has found a wooly bear.

LINDA: Oooh look everyone. A bear.

SUZE: Keep it lovey. A friend a' mine from Fulham give it me. Iss a bear.

DEREK: Ah-h-h. Kiss a lickle bear then Linda eh?

During the rest of DEREK's next speech CAROL is calling down to the boys in the street below. Her actions should be orchestrated with DEREK's words. She seems, as so often, to be full of manic, suppressed excitement . . . strung out . . . 'All free a' yer? . . . Or just 'im? . . . Well all right. . . Flat A sixf floor . . . You open it from up 'ere doncher? . . . Don' worry abaht no . . . Yeah all right you . . . you . . .'

I 'ad a mate up Cadogan Gardens. A really good mate 'e was. On'y 'e went ter fuckin' Auschtralia din' 'e? Wiv 'is Mum an' Dad. Fings 'ave definitely bin rubbish since Kevin fucked off. I mean oo wants ter know yer. No future. I tell you I'll turn inter a fuckin' gel soon. Gels. They're really 'ard is gels.

LINDA: Girls isn't 'ard. Girls is soft. Girls is sweet an' kind. Leave off a' that fuckin' bear Chrace I got it first din't I?

TRACY: 'Ey Sharon 'is eyes light up!

CAROL (*she is half-way out of the window with excitement*): Well push ver fuckin' thing 'arder cancher!

SUZE rushes at her furiously.

SUZE: Fer Chrissake gel if I ain' got enough chrouble wiv my neighbours already woch you finkin of eh? Blimey ainch yoo got no manners?

Pulling her off.

CAROL: Sorry sorry sorry sorry sorry. I'm sorry Suze I'm sorry I'm sorry O.K.? O.K.?

SHARON: Woss ver matter canch yoo fuckin' wait?

CAROL: Oh don't Sharon please Sharon please Sharon don't –

LINDA: Sticks and stones can break my bones but words will never hurt me.

DEREK: Fuck off cunt.

This amuses DEREK. *It does not amuse anyone else.* SUZE *is now at the window.*

SUZE: Iss a sticky door lovey! Ainch yoo never seen a sticky door before? Pull the knob. The knob dear. (*To the girls:*) 'E's goin' ter be a lot a fun 'en 'e? Maybe we should tempt 'is mates up an' all.

CAROL: Oh get 'im Suze go on get 'im less 'ave a look at 'im go on less 'ave a –

SHARON: Lissen Carol arter woch yoo –

CAROL: Don't *talk* abaht it. O.K.? Please. Please do not *talk* abaht it.

SHARON *has a gentle tact sometimes, perhaps strange in someone as aggressive looking as she is.*

SHARON: Fine. No problems.

SUZE: Woss up wiv vese two gels? Now. Beam up a man Captain Kirk! Woss she bin up to then that dark girl there?

She presses the buzzer. LINDA *is walking around the stage with the bear held high. She is examining its bum.*

LINDA: 'Ere Derek – look at vis bear! It pees when you squeeze it.

DEREK: Oh fuck off Linda.

SUZE: Innit a laugh. You can put nappies on it an' everyfing.

LINDA: Ahh. In't that *lovelee*!

DEREK: No it bleed'n well isn't.

LINDA: You was in nappies once.

TRACY: Still are.

SUZE: ORDER LADIES PLEASE! SHALL WE 'AVE A LITTLE BIT OF ORDER! (*She opens the door. Satirically:*) A lovely young boy oo 'as taken a fancy to one a yoo young gels is come against us, an' seein' as 'e appears to 'ave follered yoo all the way from bleed'n Parsons Green can we make an attempt to be'ave like young ladies an' not spit or shove chewin' gum dahn our knickers. O.K.? We wanna show 'im a good time do we not?

SHARON: Well yoo do an' no mistake doncher darlin'?

CAROL: I'm sca - ared . . .

SUZE, *oblivious to the needle from* SHARON *pulls back the door sharply, hiding herself behind it and blowing a*

fanfare as she does so. Behind the door is revealed STEVE, *an attractive young lad of sixteen or eighteen. Neat, nervous and with a precariously acquired bravura manner. When he doesn't use this – which is for quite a lot of the time, he is clearly, tolerably sweet natured.*

SHARON: Well well well. A real live man. John Wayne is come among us.

CAROL: Well. Woch yoo wanna come follerin' us like that for you schoopid lit'l boy donch yoo know no better an' wot you mean by it I *do* not know I am sure I never saw such a thing in my life I never did so 'elp me God gawpin' arter us like we was dogs or sunnink fer *Chrissake* woch yoo mean by it I really don't know. (*Shaking.*) Giss a jrink Sharon.

SHARON: She likes 'im.

SUZE: I'm Suze. Woss yer name lovey? This is my place.

STEVE: Nice. Steve.

SUZE: Still at school are yer?

STEVE: In an' out. You know. Chrainin' I am.

SUZE: Don't I know lovey. You'll 'ave whiskey woncher like yore friend there?

STEVE: Yeah. (*Tough guy.*) 'Bells.' (*The girls fall about.*)

SHARON: 'Ark at 'im. (*Joke tough guy.*) 'Bells.' (*Up to him.*) 'Spose she ain't got no Bells then? Will ve entire world collapse will it? Will you 'ave to 'ave tea instead? You amuse me mate.

STEVE: 'E yore boy then?

SUZE: I ain't that far gone am I lovey?

DEREK: I'm one a' the girls.

STEVE: Oh. Nice. Ta.

SUZE *is serving drinks, still in a haze of satisfaction at being the entertainer.*)

Voss ver dark one's name?

SHARON: Dark one? Dark one? 'Ark at 'im. You ain' in no fairground now son. This ain't jus' pick'n'mix you know. We is people in vis room mate not just spare. Eh? Dark one indeed. 'Is name is Derek.

STEVE: Yore a joker aincher?

SHARON: I'm Ten Ton Tessie Wiv the 'Eadlights on. I'm Supergirl. I'm a Man

Slicer. I'm Mrs Mean I am an' my profession is cuttin' men ter size. (*Flicking his tie.*) You get ma meanin' lit'l man. Huh?

Despite the fact that she's sending up this sort of behaviour, STEVE *can't help but respond.*

STEVE: Steady!

SHARON: Steady!

STEVE: Watch it!

SHARON: Watch it! (*To the rest of the girls:*) You ever seen men do that girls? 'Watch it!' 'Steady!' Like we was dogs or sunnink. But my Mum always sez you wanna watch a good fight you go an' see two gels. No-one fights like two gels. Fact. Jus' remember that – (*Joke male again.*) Lit'l man!

SUZE: Leave it aht gels. Less 'ave a lit'l conversation. Carm along. This is Auntie Suze's innit? Everybody's got ter get along right? Less 'ave some inchroductions shall we? Less get ter know each uvver. Put Stephen at 'is ease eh?

She vamps STEVE. *By no means putting him at his ease.*

TRACY: 'Er name's Carol I'm Tracy thass Linda wiv ver Bear an' thass Derek an' thass Suze wot we met ternight an' that one wiv 'er 'and on yore collar is Sharon an' she's boss incha Sharon?

SHARON: I am in charge of entertainments!

STEVE: Carol wot?

SUZE: Oh we can see the way 'is inclinations are tendin' can't we girls? We can see which one 'e's got 'is eye on can't we now? Go on love she won't bite.

SHARON: You 'eard wot ver lady said young man 'ave a shot. Give it a whirl. Walk up walk up 'ave a bash. Woch yoo usually do when you're . . . you know . . . you know . . . chattin' 'em up a bit . . . eh?

Very slowly STEVE *is approaching* CAROL.

Carm on carm on. Now woch yoo say?

STEVE: 'Ullo!

SHARON: Piss off. You go –

She shoulders STEVE *out of the way. But her anger is directed as much at* CAROL *for allowing all this to happen.*

Got a light love?

CAROL: *Please* Sharon!

SHARON: Got a light?

Finally CAROL *turns to her friend.* SHARON *does a cave man assault on her. Larky. But* CAROL *is upset, not amused by it.*

CAROL: STOP IT CANCHER? YOU SAID YOU WASN'T GONNA FUCKIN' MENTION THAT DINCHER? FER GAWD'S SAKE LEAVE OFF OF IT EH? EH?

SHARON: Sorree. Sorree!

STEVE: Blimey. Lesbians.

SHARON is still holding CAROL.

LINDA: Woss lesbians?

SUZE: Bad women deary.

DEREK: Vey're a team. Lesbians United. A foopball team. In Scotland. I fink.

TRACY: Oh fuck off an' play wiv' yore bear.

SHARON has broken from CAROL. STEVE *approaches slowly.*

STEVE: 'Ullo.

CAROL: 'Ullo.

Everyone's watching them.

STEVE: Fancy a jrink?

CAROL: Got one already fanks.

STEVE: Oh. (*Pause.*) Yeh. (*Pause.*) Where you from then?

CAROL: Brixton.

STEVE: Oh yeh.

CAROL: Caulfield estate.

STEVE: I don't know that.

CAROL: No. Nobody does.

STEVE: Nice is it?

CAROL: No. (*Her poise breaks into giggles.*) Fuckin' smells dunnit.

The girls break up with laughter. SUZE *disapproves. Her attitudes change now there's a man in the room.*

SUZE: Very nice I must say.

SHARON: Well it fuckin' does though Suze. Romeo 'ere won't mind us pointin' that aht will yer Romeo? It fuckin' smells. Chroo. Factually chroo. No pub no lift no ball games no winders no grass no nuffink. Iss like a battleship on'y I never arst ter join ver Navy know wot I mean?

SUZE: You know wot I'm talkin' about my girl.

SHARON: I 'aven't the faintest idea woch yore talkin' abaht you wanna know. Unless you fink Romeo 'ere is so fuckin' sensitive 'e's goin' ter curl up an' die becos ver one 'e loves knows a few words 'e don't. Blimey woch yoo on abaht anyway?

SUZE: Some men do not like to hear a woman swear.

SHARON: Some men do not fuckin' like to 'ear a woman *speak* do they? In ver which case swearin' might not be such a fuckin' bad idea. An' wot I wanner know is why yoo –

STEVE *comes up. 'Sorting out the women'.*

STEVE: You know yore chrouble. Yore bitter you are. Becos of 'ow you look. Yeh. (*An attempt at psychology.*) Now in fact you ain't bad lookin'. In fact. You grow yore 'air a bit an' stop walkin' arahn wiv yore fumbs in yore belt you might be all right.

SHARON: Joo fink so?

STEVE: Honest. Yoo might do O.K.

SHARON: Reely. (*Mock thrilled.*) Might I get a boy all a' my own?

STEVE: You might.

SHARON: An' might he . . . you know . . .

STEVE: Yeh.

SHARON: Might I reely get a look at 'is . . . you know . . . 'is . . . you know wot . . . ?

STEVE: You never know.

SHARON: A real live one.

STEVE: Real live one.

SHARON: Real enormous bloody great one.

STEVE: Lissen –

SHARON: Absolutely huge colossal gigantic enormous terrifically amazin'ly large one.

STEVE: Look –

SHARON: WELL MIGHT I? MIGHT I GET A BUTCJERS' AT 'IS FANTASTICALLY CENTRALLY DOMINATING VIBRANT GIGANTIC 'UGE COLOSSAL AMAZIN' AN' STUPENDOUS BLEED'N ORGAN? EH?

STEVE: YES I SUPPOSE YOU MIGHT IF YOU ARST NICELY!

SHARON: WELL LESS 'AVE A LOOK AT IT THEN!

And with a whoop of joy she springs on him. They wrestle.

STEVE: Get off! Get fuckin' off!

They roll on the floor.

TRACY: Ain't she a case eh?

CAROL: SHARON!

SUZE: Well fer Gawd's sweet –

STEVE: GET OFF!

But she's managed to get her hand down his trousers. The struggle ceases. SHARON sits up.

SHARON: Disastrous. Waste a' time.

SUZE: Well if there's goin' ter be much more a' this then –

SHARON: It's gone inter 'ibernation. Early.

TRACY: Joo pull it Sharon?

STEVE: Fer Gawd's sake!

This is all reasonably good-humoured.

SHARON: I reckon iss shy.

STEVE: It is.

She bends over his trousers.

SHARON: 'Ullo' . . . 'Ullo-o' . . . lit'l blo-oke! . . . don' be nervous . . . the coast's clear . . . there's on'y 'unjreds a ravenous women out 'ere all after a bit . . . come alo-ong . . . come alo-ong . . . (*To the girls.*) It cannot be tempted from its 'ole.

SUZE: Well I 'ope we're not gonner spend ve 'ole evenin' bein' bleed'n vulgar. If there's one fing I can't stand iss fuckin' 'orseplay. You'll be on ter bleed'n nudism next you will. Gawd I 'ate all that. Iss like the delicatessen innit?

SHARON (*jokey*): Be nach'ral Suze. Be real. Be like me.

SUZE: Well you leave off of your friend cancher? Fer 'eaven's sake you –

SHARON: Lissen I look arter 'er O.K.? I look arter 'er. I ain' 'avin' 'er messed abaht I'm a friend O.K.? I'm 'er chaperone.

STEVE: You ain't no chaperone. Yore a fuckin' thug yoo are.

Getting up. Rubbing himself

I'll 'ave ter 'av the old Elastoplast on this I will. Put it back in ver fuckin' fridge. Blimey. Funny friends you got Carol.(*He sits by her.*) Less off shall we?

CAROL: Nah. I can't –

STEVE: This ain't no use.

SHARON: Read and learn gels. A man is plottin' to pick off one of our number. 'E is bein' wiley. An' extremely polite an' all. But once 'e's aht of 'ere it'll be grope grope grope like a fuckin' mechanical shovel it will be, like a Dalek or sunnink.

CAROL: We could dance or sunnink.

STEVE: Oh fer –

SUZE: Well now thass a *nice* idea.

SHARON: Oh Gawd.

SUZE: Yore a killjoy you are aincher.

STEVE: O.K. Less dance.

TRACY: Vere's cassettes an' everyfing 'ere.

SUZE: Put on the Beatles love. Put on a bit a' dance music.

TRACY: Oo?

SUZE: Blimey don' tell me you never 'eard a' the Beatles lovey? Vey was famous. Vey was the most famous people in the world was the Beatles.

TRACY: 'Ere they are. (*Studying the cassette. Shrugging.*) Might as well give 'em a whirl.

She puts it on. 'Revolution' plays. CAROL *and* STEVE *get up.* CAROL *dances. So does* STEVE.

SHARON: Oooh 'en 'e masculine. 'En 'e decisive. Stickin' 'is leg up in ve air like a spaniel at a lamppost.

He continues to dance.

I don' like the way men dance. I fink iss reely schoopid. Wigglin' their bums arahnd like everyone was lookin' at them. I mean all men are fuckin' fit for is gettin' in ver coal reely. Look at 'im. Reckons we should bow down an' fuckin' worship don' 'e?

SUZE: You one a' them burn yore bra merchants are yer Sharon?

SHARON: I ain't got no bra. I let 'em swing. An' I put steel tips on ver fuckin' front don' I?

SUZE: If a woman is beautiful let her show it – thass wot I say.

SHARON: Show wot though thass the question innit Suze? 'Er legs? 'Er 'eart? 'Er brain? Eh? Go it Sambo – kick yer legs up. You are dancin' fuckin' dreadful you are. You should be out doin' sunnink reely masculine an' –

STEVE: LEAVE OFF CANCHER? EH? WOSS GOT INTER YOU?

SHARON: I was raped. When I was two I was raped by my ol' man. Then I was raped by my prim'ry school teacher. Then I was raped by ten lollipop men on me way ter school. Then I was raped by the 'ead of a large London comprehensive oose name I am not allowed ter reveal on account proceedin's are now bein' taken against 'im. Then I was raped by a Careers Officer. An' finally I was sexually assaulted by ve owner of a garridge on Brixton 'Ill.

STEVE *has stopped dancing.*

TRACY: Sharon wan'ed ter work in a garridge. They woun't let 'er.

SHARON: They don' approve a' women mechanics. They want women on fuckin' Pirelli calendars they do. Or women on birfday cakes wiv sugar 'eads, or women fuckin' doin' their dinners an' –

CAROL: Reely Sharon I'm on'y chryin' to 'ave a dance ain' I? Is that so much to ask please I mean why joo 'ave ter spoil fings every time I chry an' 'ave a lit'l amusement I do not know sometimes I do not know why I bovver ter 'ang arahnd wiv you frankly I *do* not know if you'd like ter *know* Sharon.

SHARON: You know.

TRACY: When Carol was in –

CAROL: SHUT UP!

STEVE: Fuckin' jragons you are. I'm off out.

SUZE: Sit by me lovey.

He crosses towards her.

LINDA: Oo look an' ole cupboard full a' them.

She has been on the prowl and discovered a vast pile of wombles, gooks and fluffy toys at the back of the room.

SUZE: Play 'ousey 'ousey dear. There my animals in' they. My boyfriend give 'em to me.

SHARON: All the way from fuckin' Tehran.

SUZE: Yore reely bad mannered you are. I shall –

SHARON: Call the Law?

SUZE: Oh give over. 'Ere lovey. Sit by Auntie. 'Ave a Dun'ill.

SHARON: Gecha toys aht Linda. Give 'em cups a' tea. Wipe their fuckin' bums for 'em. Send 'em ter University. Go on. Knit 'em lit'l sweaters an' give 'em Weetabix. In a few fuckin' years you'll be practisin' on ver reel fing. Blimey – you might even be tuckin' Derek up at night.

DEREK: Piss off!

SUZE: You reely are very bitter abaht sunnink incher gel? I'm beginnin' ter fink young Stephen 'ere is right.

CAROL: Leave off of 'er Suze.

SUZE: She ain't doin' you no favours lovey.

CAROL: Oh favours? Woss favours? She done me plenty.

SHARON: I done 'er plenty. When she –

CAROL: *Sharon!*

SHARON: On'y teasin'.

STEVE: You been inside then?

CAROL: Not ver place you mean I ain't.

LINDA: Derek – 'elp me get this lot aht willyer?

DEREK: Wocher goin' ter do wiv em?

LINDA: Put 'em on chairs. In a circle.

DEREK: Oh fuck.

SHARON: Will you look at them two?

STEVE *has sat by* SUZE.

SUZE: If the Good Lord 'ad intended us ter be garage mechanics Stephen 'e woun't a' given us these beautiful breasts an' this lovely complexion an' these shapely thighs an' all vat rubbish would 'e nah?

STEVE: I suppose not.

SUZE: Some fings are a woman's business an' uvvers are best left ter the menfolk. Know wot I mean lovey?

STEVE: Well men is obviously better at liftin' fings ain't they? 'Eavy fings.

SHARON: Yeh. Like two year old children and bags a'shoppin' an' –

STEVE: I *mean*. Like bags a' coal. An' wardrobes. An' dinin'-room tables. An' blocks a' concrete.

SHARON: You ain't talkin' abaht men son. You are talkin' abaht fuckin' fork lift chrucks you are. Blimey.

Pause.

You remind me a' my ol' man you do. 'Leave this ter me Sal' 'e used ter say ter my ol' lady, 'leave this ter me'. Well she left ver sink to 'im an' it blocked up she left ver car to 'im an' 'e jrove into a wall she left the money to 'im an' 'e wen' an' fuckin' spent it din't 'e? Couple a' gits.

STEVE: Wot is up wiv you?

SHARON: I was on'y runner up in the Miss Lambef All Comers On'y Slags May Apply Competition. It was won by a girl wiva broken nose an' deformed ears on account she give it ter one a' the judges. No. I tell a lie. I am not able to 'ave a child on account my womb is situated be'ind my right ear'ole an' every time a sperm gets near it it goes inter terminal shock. No. I tell a lie. I am un'appy becos I am all 'orrible an' ugly an' cannot wear partyjresses like ve ovver girls an' 'ave ter walk arahnd in a suit of armour ter get people ter whistle at me. No. I tell a lie. Women are known ter be inconsistent. I am jealous of my loving young friend 'ere, Carol, on account she gets all ver boys and I end up wiv ver bridge rolls. No. I tell a lie. She ends up wiv ver boys *an* ver fuckin' bridge roll. No. I tell a –

CAROL: STOP IT SHARON!

SHARON: Well isn't it chroo? Eh? Isn't it?

CAROL: No.

SHARON: Oh I dunno. Maybe I wan'ed ter be a fuckin' garridge mechanic. Maybe thass all it is. Maybe thass all. I dunno. It ain't much ter ask though is it? It ain't a lot. It ain't as if I was askin' ter be Jackie

Onassis or Margaret bleed'n Thatcher is it? I jus' wan' ter mend cars. Now is that a lot to ask?

STEVE *gets up.*

STEVE: Less go Carol eh?

CAROL: No.

STEVE: Woch yoo wanna 'ang arahnd wiv 'er for?

CAROL: She's my friend in't she?

STEVE: Some friend she is to you. Won't let you dance won't let you talk. Blimey. She might be yore bleed'n muvver ver way she carries on. Nah. You comin'?

CAROL: No. Sorry. But no.

SHARON: See Stevie boy? Female company still 'as charms fer our friend Carol. Dunnit? Now 'ow can vis be? Maybe she jus' don' wan' any 'eavy weights lifted at the moment.

STEVE: A man can do more than lift 'eavy weights.

SHARON: Tell me more Stephen.

STEVE: A man 'as got a bigger brain. Gen'rally.

SUZE: I'm sure thass chroo. I ferget me own name I do.

SHARON *crosses to* STEVE.

SHARON: Ah. This is it gels. Ain't we in luck. We 'ave got a male brain on ver premises. Look at it. Fumpin' away be'ind 'is 'air. You can 'ear it cancher? Boo ber der boom boo ber der boom. Leakin' intelligence all over ver room. Iss in vere somewhere – like a great big, wet cauliflower. We are in luck aren't we ladies? If we wanna know anyfing wot our useless lit'l girl-sized brains can't figger out we better ask it.

Shouts at his temples.

'OW MANY BEANS MAKE FIVE? Oo won ver Second World War?

SUZE: A man's brains aren't 'is most important feature dear.

LINDA: Iss whevver 'e'll make a good provider innit Derek?

DEREK: I dunno Linda. Giss a break anyway. I ain't taken my fuckin' C.S.E. yet 'ave I?

TRACY: Woss 'is most important feature Carol?

CAROL: I like a man wiv a good chest on him.

SUZE: Me too dear.

STEVE: You come ter ver right ajress then Carol.

CAROL: Less 'ave a look at it then.

STEVE: 'Ello 'ello 'ello.

SHARON: Go on. Giss a lit'l look at them tits a' yores Stevie boy.

STEVE (*to* CAROL): I do Japanese exercises.

SHARON: Oooh. Nice.

CAROL: Less 'ave a look then.

STEVE: All steamed up are yer?

CAROL: I might be.

SUZE: Romance is in ve air.

SHARON: There's a name fer it but it ain't romance.

STEVE: 'Ere goes.

SHARON: An' 'e is takin' off 'is shirt. This ten stone weakling from Parson's Green is actually takin' off 'is shirt an' all of us 'ere askin' the million dollar question ' 'as 'e got a vest on?' Well '*as* 'e got a vest on, and the answer is . . . (STEVE *has taken off his shirt.*)No 'e ain't. An' 'e ain't got a chest neiver.

SUZE: Ooh inch yoo tanned. Fer winter.

STEVE: They got a lamp. In ver gym.

CAROL: Not *bad*.

LINDA: Go on Derek – you take yore shirt off an' all.

DEREK: Fuck off cunt.

SHARON: Oh yes. *Yes*. It is startin' ter become clear ter me. I am beginnin' to understand it all. Oh yes. I mean I was 'avin' problems but this does 'elp. I mean look girls. You can see now cancher. Vis is why men is superior ter gels innit. I mean this woch yoo might call 'ard evidence. Notice the 'air under the arms an' ve elbows specially designed fer frowin' cricket balls schraight. 'Ere . . .

Walking round him as if he were an exhibit in a museum.

'Ere we can see ve shoulders specially for liftin' sacks a' coal, an' the cares a' the world an' brides over thresh'olds an' thresh'olds theirselves most likely and vis little lump 'ere is the bicep or wife-beating fitment you place the wife over yore knee anj yoo go – (*Ape man voice.*) 'Leave this to me!' (*Still walking round him.*) Not a lot else to notice at this stage. The neck which smells like a bowl a' dogfood an' ve ears be'ind which it is chraditional not to wash. 'I like,' as my ol' man sez, 'a man oo smells like a man' i.e. fuckin' jreadful –

STEVE: Leave me ears alone.

SHARON: Well you still ain't shown me son wot there is so fuckin' wonderfully *special* abaht bein' a man.

STEVE (*leer*): Yore lookin' in ver wrong place incher?

SHARON: We'll get there son we'll get back to that. In style.

SUZE: A woman, lovey, jus' *needs* a man an' vere it is. I mean a man may be a bastard to 'cr see? A man may do ver most jreadful cruel fings. I mean my first husband used ter tie me up an' frow fuckin' plates at me. 'E did. But. A woman *needs* 'im see?

SHARON: You needed ver crockery didjer Suze? You was well inter that was you?

SUZE: It is bleed'n 'opeless chryin' ter explain anyfing ter you.

TRACY: Men got penises I suppose.

CAROL: You can Sharon. You can want it an' not want it. Iss woch yoo want – I mean everyfing in ver world woch yoo want an 'en again it ain't.

SHARON: Well you oughter know all abaht that Carol.

STEVE: Was you raped or sunnink?

CAROL: Yeh I was attacked by a gorilla in ver zoo. All night 'e done ter me. Free 'unjred an' twenny-eight times 'e done it ter me, which is ver world record even fer a gorilla. An' in ver mornin' 'e sez 'Well that was very nice. Now fer sunnink completely different' an' 'e on'y offers me a banana don't 'e?

SHARON: She did not accept. She'd all the fruit she needed.

CAROL: Anyway 'is missus come back

from ver cage nex' door.

TRACY: Mrs Gorilla.

SHARON: An' she sez –

CAROL: 'George where you bin?'

STEVE: Look I'll tell yer this. When I gech yer alone then we'd be all right see? We'd be O.K. No man can talk ter no woman when vere's fifty ovver slags peerin' over 'is shoulder an' yackin' away an' gettin' up 'is nose can 'e now?

SHARON: Oh Stephen where you gonna take 'er then? Mount fuckin' Athos are yer? Mars is it? I dunno whevver you noticed it son but on this planet vere is a considerable number a' women abaht – in buses an' 'at – you must a' seen 'em. You know – big black ones wiv shoppin' baskets an' lit'l blond ones wiv eyes like pandas an' grey ones wiv abaht ten kids an' ones stitched up wiv corsets an' faces like Major Generals. Carm on son. Where you goin' ter take 'er?

STEVE: Where vere ain't women yowlin' rahnd in a fuckin' pack you wanna know.

SHARON: Ah now vis is ve on'y diff'rence son. In 'ere it may be all gels –

DEREK: Do you mind?

SHARON: Out there iss all men. Iss all packs an' packs son innit an' you dealt yoreself inter ver wrong dincher tonight eh? Dincher?

She takes his shirt. Crosses to the window.

Ah. Talkin' a' packs. Yor mates is still there. (*She holds up the shirt.*) ONE NIL TO US LADS! (*She chucks it out.*)

STEVE: Oi thass my shirt!

SHARON: Plenty more ter come in't there?

STEVE: I'm not takin' nuffink else off. Blimey.

CAROL: I changed me mind. I gone off chests.

STEVE: Oh 'ave you?

CAROL: Yeh. I'm inter legs now.

SUZE: Oh I like a leg lovey. I like a good masculine leg. I like a plump hairy leg wiv a knee in the middle an' lit'l wirey 'airs on it all the way up. Oh I like that. I 'ad a boyfriend from Malta once 'oo 'ad the most incredibly 'airy legs. 'E was like an insect, But I was mad fer 'im.

SHARON: Is there any part a' the male body you ain't particularly inchrested in Suze?

SUZE: I can't say as I like bottoms. My first 'usband 'ad a rarver large bottom as a result of which 'e was known as Arse'ole. (*Realising she is being sent up.*) Lissen my gel you chry an' mock me an' I'll 'ave you.

STEVE: That or you'll change yore ways eh?

SUZE: Look leave off a' me eh?

SHARON: Now all I'm chyrin' ter do is make you fink a lit'l. But isn't it painful? Oh isn't it fuckin' painful?

LINDA: I like legs.

TRACY: Me too.

CAROL: Anyone else fer legs?

STEVE (*Another attempt at psychology*): I know wot Carol – that Sharon a' yores sets yoo against men. When I come in 'ere you was all –

SHARON: Legs Stephen. We all like legs. Off wiv 'em.

STEVE: My legs ain't me best feature.

SHARON: Legs.

ALL THE GIRLS: LEGS! LEGS! LEGS!

SHARON: 1-2-3

ALL THE GIRLS: CHROUSERS DOWN

They are all getting up and converging on him. Still reasonably jokey.

STEVE: Steady on gels!

SHARON: 2-3-4 WOT IS IT WE'RE WAITIN' FOR?

ALL THE GIRLS: 5-6-7 CHROUSERS!

STEVE: LOOK –

SHARON: ACTION!

And they fall on him with whoops of joy. He struggles back. Much giggling and laughing and then finally a pair of jeans are waved aloft. Only DEREK and SUZE have not joined in.

SUZE: Well. I was goin' ter spend a quiet evenin' wiv a bottle a' Campari.

DEREK: They are bad them girls. They're bullies in fact.

The group breaks away from him. SHARON has got the trousers.

TRACY: Oooh in 'e got lovely knickers.

CAROL: Briefs they are. Like fer sport.

SHARON: One pair a' chrousers gels. One pair a' denim jeans. (*Going to the window.*) Shall we show them to the waiting crowd? (*At the window.*) 'Ere they are boys! Very useful! Grab a load a' this!

STEVE: OH NOT OUT THE WINDER!

But she has thrown them.

SUZE: Don' less get carried away nah gels. We –

CAROL: Oi! Cop a load a' this. (*She has found a magazine on the floor that dropped out of STEPHEN's pocket.*) Oh blimey. This is all right. Look at *this*!

STEVE: Leave that aht of it!

CAROL (*reads*): 'Susan is a twenty-free year old video typist from Beverley Hills oo likes the outdoor life. We thought she looked just perfect in the snow capped mountains above 'er ski-ing 'ome in . . . ' Blimey.

SHARON: Less 'ave a look.

STEVE: Leave me magazine alone cancher?

TRACY: Cor!

SHARON: In't they 'uge!

TRACY: Vey inject theirselves. Wiv plastic.

CAROL: Oooh they're all swingin'!

SHARON: In't she got a tiny bum though. Iss ver size of a fuckin' peanut. You woun't stay on a fuckin' chair wiv vat bum woujer?

STEVE: You'd stay on a chair though wouncer Fatso? You'd stay on a fuckin' church steeple you would.

SHARON: Come over 'ere an' say that.

STEVE: No.

CAROL: Oooh look this one's stickin' 'er bum in ve air.

TRACY: In't that one rude though. Dead rude that is.

SHARON: Stephen . . . joo . . . you know

. . . 'ave a look at these and . . . you know . . . ?

She mimes wanking.

STEVE: Shut up!

SHARON: No. Do yer . . . do yer . . . you *know* . . .

STEVE: So wot if I do?

TRACY: Makes yer go blind.

DEREK: Doesn't.

SHARON: You oughter know Derek.

LINDA: Derek don't do nuffink like vat do yer Derek?

DEREK: None a' yore business.

LINDA: When we're married you won't do vat. I won' lecher.

DEREK: Oo said anyfing abaht marriage?

LINDA: I did. 'Old vis Womble.

STEVE (*trying to force an alliance with DEREK*): Marriage is wot they want mate. Tie yer down wiv a couple a' kids. All they fuckin' want ter do mate. Yeah. Don' get involved. They take yer chrousers off an' frow 'em aht the winder. Not worf it.

SHARON: Now you watch yore step Geronimo. We are lookin' at yore lovely magazine.

SUZE: I don' see woss so funny abaht a girl doin' nude modellin'. In fact I done ve odd pose in my time if you wanner know. I done a tableau on a rug. For friends. When jrunk.

SHARON: Wiv a giant banana!

SUZE: Reely you are sick you are. The female body can be very beautiful. It can be a very lovely fing.

SHARON: Yeh an' it can be bleed'n awful an' all when iss done up like a dog's dinner wiv titts the size a' soop plates bein' pored over by some geezer in a mac. . . 'This is Julie she is a computer operative from 'Ighbury an' 'er 'obby is makin' boats out a matchsticks which is why we showed 'er wiv 'er fanny 'angin' aht of 'er chrousers jus' ter leave you wankers aht there in no doubt as ter wot she's fuckin' got.' (*Spits.*) They ain't women they're fuckin' dolls they are. Like ve ones filled wiv water.

SUZE: Photographs of a woman –

SHARON: Photographs of a fuckin' woman is lies in the main Suze. Jesus fuckin' Christ Suze take a look rahn yore wall Suze. All these birds you got 'ere swoonin' arahnd an' –

SUZE: Beggin' yore pardon young lady but vere is on'y *one* woman pitchered in vis room an' I'll thank yoo ter be a lit'l more polite when you make reference to 'er on account that woman is none uvver than myself in oose flat you now are an' 'arf of oose fuckin' whiskey you 'ave poured dahn yore young froat in ver last quarter of an hour thank *you*!

SHARON: HOORAY!

Falling about.

Hooray gels! Woch yoo aht ter give yerself Suze? Fuckin' schizophrenia. Woch yoo at eh? Lookin' like this an' lookin' like that an' blimey ainch yoo got a fuckin' face a' yore own oh Christ it riles me you know that? It riles me ter see you gawpin' arahnd like that well look at 'em gels look at 'em where's the fuckin' woman I can't see the fuckin' *woman*!

Starting to rip the pictures down.

SUZE: YOU STOP THAT YOU RUDE LIT'L BITCH YOU STOP THAT AT ONCE OR I'LL –

SHARON: YOU'LL WOT? CANCH YOO FUCKIN' USE YORE 'EAD! SOMEONE'S CHRYIN' TER GIVE YOO AN EJUCATION 'ERE BUCH YOO AIN'T LISTENIN' ARE YER? FER GAWD'S SAKE! GAWD AN' OOS THIS WIV IS MORNIN' SUIT? THIS 'USBAND NUMBER ONE? BLIMEY AN' 'ERE WE ARE AGAIN MARRIED! BLEED'N MARRIED! DINCH YOO NEVER LEARN SUZE? LISSEN!

STEVE: EVERYONE'S LISTENIN' BUCH YOO SLAG! YOU 'EAR! EVERYONE WANTS A QUIET AN' A LIT'L ENJOYMENT BUCH YOO YOO 'EAR?

Getting up. Unaware of how ludicrous he looks witout his trousers.

'S jus' you chrin' ter keep me away from yore mate. 'Cos yore sick or jealous or you done sunnink to 'er or someone done sunnink to 'er *I* don't know but it's all down ter you far as I can see this is an' in the meanwhile I'll fank you fer my magazine an' my chrousers.

SHARON: Yore chrousers is aht the winder son. An' donch yoo stick yore oar in 'tween me an' Carol. We got our understandin' see? An' I wouldn't expect you ter fuckin' under*stand*.

STEVE: Oh I'm goin' ter understand slag. I'm gonna more than understand. I'm goin' ter fuckin' learn yore lit'l understan' off by 'eart. I'm goin' ter get my oar an' my eyes an' my mouf an' my teef an' my 'ole fuckin' body inter yore understandin' before this night's aht. Slag.

CAROL: Why is it quarrel quarrel quarrel eh? Why can't we be friends eh? Why is it all this arguin'?

TRACY: An' talkin' a bodies. 'E ain' took 'is undies off yet.

CAROL: Oooh!

SHARON: Observe gels the legs of a man.

Walking round him.

Very useful for climbin' up the ladders of success an' kickin' women off of it. As in ver case a' my ol' lady oo spends 'er time cleanin'. She cleans everyfing does my ol' lady. Britich Oxygen, United Dairies the B.B. fuckin' C an' usually after the hours a' darkness, which is why 'er legs do not 'ave this shapely look on account she spends so much fuckin' time on 'er knees. Note also the back a' the lower leg, extra special built fer runnin' away, kneein' enemies in the groin an' winchin' over custom built bits a plastic like Lulu 'ere from Golders Green. (*Close to him.*) Ter me yore the men up West oo told my Mum she could 'ave twenty pee a week or whatever they pay 'er, yore the men I see on the telly night arter fuckin' night goin' 'Do 'ave a Cointreau?' yore the great fat face a' my ol' man sayin' 'Leave vis ter me! Leave vis ter me!' Yore every fucker I ever seen stampin' his way frough the world aht there an' dumpin' Carol in the –

STEVE: Ah ah.

CAROL: Now you gone an' fuckin' done it aincher?

SUZE: Woss up love? Some boy lech yer dahn did 'e?

STEVE: We ain' all bastards you know. Some of us are quite recognisable 'uman –

SHARON: I DON' WANNA 'EAR ABAHT YORE RECORD FER GOOD BE'AVIOUR SONNY. I AM REALLY NOT INCHRESTED! YOU 'EAR?

STEVE: Wot was it Carol? Did –

SHARON: SHE 'AD A BABY THASS WOT IT WAS SHE 'AD A FUCKIN BABY O.K? THASS ALL. NUFFINK SPECTACULAR SHE 'AD A BABY. IT 'APPENS EVERY DAY OR 'ADN'T YOO NOTICED. ON'Y ON ACCOUNT SHE WAS A LIT'L BIT ON THE YOUNG SIDE SHE GIVE IT AWAY. SHE GIVE IT TO THE WORLD WILDLIFE FUND OR CANCER RESEARCH OR JOHN LEWIS'S OR SOME FUCKIN' FING I CAN'T REMEMBER BUT SHE GIVE IT AWAY O.K?

SUZE: Oh LOVEY!

SHARON: SHUT UP SHUT UP SHUT UP CANCHER?

Pause.

No-one come ter see 'er on'y me. No-one. Boy never fuckin' come did 'e? No-one took 'er cards or flowers or letters or booze or fuckin' shampoo on'y me an' my ol' lady. An' all rahnd 'er there's these plastic women 'oo make the right noises an' wear the right 'air an' vey're laden wiv cards an' 'usbands an' they got these babies in lit'l plastic buckets an' they're grinnin' grinning' grinning' an' the men are grinnin' an' everyone's 'appy an' dahn ve end a' the ward there's me an' my ol' lady an' Carol an' it doesn't add up does it? It doesn't making fuckin' sense.

SUZE: Children is a woman's vocation ter my mind lovey. When I 'ad Jerry I –

SHARON: Will you shut up abaht wot women's vocation is please? Far as I can see yore fuckin' vocation is fiver-a-night tricks yore vocation is. I don' wanner 'ear abaht yore vocation an' I don' wanner 'ear abaht 'is vocation neiver an' 'ow 'e was kind to 'is Mum an' 'e's goin' ter raise two point four fuckin' children an' ponce arahnd in a wolly jersey buildin' 'em shelves an' scurryin' off ter some factory ter gavver 'em nuts an' say 'Leave this ter me darlin'! Leave this ter me!' I wanner 'ear abaht me an' Carol sittin' in that 'ospital 'an we didn't 'av no nannies no cars no minks no 'obbies no guns no know-'ow we 'ad fuck all jus' me an' Carol an' this lit'l fing in a plastic bucket.

CAROL: 'E was a boy Sharon. 'E was a boy. An' I didn't want 'im. OK? An' I didn't even give 'im a name O.K? So leave off abaht it. Leave off.

But she is crying.

STEVE: Yeh. Leave off of 'er cancher?

SHARON: NO I CAN'T! AN' I CAN'T LEAVE OFF A' YOU NEIVER MISTER!

STEVE: OH! AN' WOCH YOO PLANNIN' ON THEN?

SUZE: YEH? FER GAWD'S SAKE OO JOO FINK YOU ARE EH? WOCH YOU PLANNING ON EH?

SHARON has the whiskey bottle in her hand.

SHARON: THIS!

She breaks the bottle against the cupboard.

Knickers off sexy.

TRACY: Fun an' ga-ames!

LINDA: 'Ey Sharon –

SHARON: We 'ave come ter the star performer gels. This is G.H.Q. This is where the action 'appens. This is the main number. This is wot we never reely get a good look at. This is 'my business'.

Moving to him. Everyone tense. Watching her.

I seen it in a magazine once but not enough of it. I don' fink we seen enough of it. I fink we should get ter see it on chrains an' buses an' chubes an' in ver middle a' Trafalgar Square an' on ver telly an' I 'fink we should see blokes flashin' their things an' saying' 'Come on in ter Bird's Eye Country'. I fink we should se an' 'ole lot more a' the winkle an' then maybe we'll be favoured wiv a noo race a' plastic men an' the plastic men can bugger off wiv ver plastic women an' maybe there'll be one or two actual people wot don't come apart when yoo 'old 'em up ter the light. People, people I look everywhere for people an' all I see is dummies 'oldin' 'ands an sayin' 'love love love' like it was fuckin' Christmas.

CAROL (*strung up giggle*): 'E's frightened I'll recognise 'im.

STEVE: Leave it aht Carol.

CAROL: Use ver fuckin' bottle on 'im. Go on carve 'im up, give 'im a taste of 'is fuckin' medicine. Go on . . . follerin' us . . . I don' know . . . boys all the fuckin' same . . . go on give 'im a taste. Go on jus' chry 'im –

STEVE: Carol –

CAROL: Sorry sorry sorry sorry.

STEVE: I mean not every bleed'n man jrops women in it nah does 'e? I mean we ain't all –

SHARON: Off!

TRACY: Off!

ALL GIRLS: 1 – 2 – 3 – 4 WOT IS IT WE'RE WAITIN' FOR?

LINDA: Is it a lit'l one then?

STEVE: FER CRYIN' AHT LOUD! I NEVER GOT NO GIRL PREGNANT! BLIMEY! I MEAN ENOUGH'S ENOUGH INNIT? I NEVER EVEN GOT CLOSE ENOUGH TO A FUCKIN' GIRL TER MAKE ER PREGNANT! I JUS' LIKE FOLLERIN' –

SHARON holds up the bottle and the magazine.

SHARON: OFF OFF OFF!

ALL GIRLS: CHROUSERS DAHN!

STEVE: WELL I FINK THIS IS VERY UNFAIR!

Pause.

I mean wot 'ave I done I'd like ter know 'part from actually exist please? I mean someone's got ter ask some girl somewhere ver time a' day 'en 'e? I mean someone, somewhere 'as got ter kind a' carry on fer Chrissake? 'Asn't 'e?

SUZE: An' as fer you wiv your 'fiver-a-night' rubbish gel I'll tell you this you're rubbish if anyone's rubbish you 'ear me? Babies? I've 'ad three fuckin' babies an' they was all took 'cos the fuckin' judge reckoned I was unfit. Gawd I'd a' liked ter seen 'im wiv a pile a' nappies. I'll tell you ahabt babies.

SHARON ignores her.

YORE RUBBISH! YORE RUBBISH! YORE RUBBISH! I TELL YOU ALL THIS ABAHT BABIES YOU NEVER 'AD ONE DIDJER? BABIES BABIES YOU DON' FUCKIN' UNDERSTAND YOU LEAVE OFF OF 'ER I MEAN I 'AD MINE IN CARE YOU KNOW. I GIVE MINE UP YOU DON' FUCKIN' KNOW!!! YOU IGNORANT BITCH!!

But SUZE's shreiking turns in upon herself and she ends, not by flying at SHARON but lacerating her own face with her nails, crying maybe until the blood comes.

SHARON: Off young man! Get 'em off!

She holds up the bottle, half satirically. What compels STEVE is as much shame and the sheer weight of women as the threat of the bottle. He starts to strip and the girls, together, in sudden high good humour – DEREK joining in as well – start to hum 'The Stripper'. STEVE plays up to it as best he can.

Ah. Ah. This is more like it. This wot we gels want an' crave for an' acksherly *lack* innit. I mean if we 'ad one a' those we'd be laughin' woun't we eh? I mean we'd all be fuckin' brain surgeons by now woun't we eh? Or in ver Cabinet – warnin' people abaht inflation an' at' eh? Oh yes. Donch yoo wish you 'ad one a' them?

DEREK: I 'ave.

LINDA: On'y yore mate Kevin borrered it din't 'e?

DEREK: Jus' 'cos I won't wiv you.

LINDA: Yore chicken thass wot.

SHARON: Oh this is *it*! The leanin' tower a' fuckin' Pisa. Amazin'. A real live organ in our power at last gels.

STEVE (*to* CAROL): Well I fought you was sensible I fought you was –

CAROL: Oh give over. I ain't lookin' anyway.

And she isn't.

SHARON: Don' be shy Carol. I fought vis was why you was makin' eyes at our young friend. Don' tell me it was becos of 'is powers a' concentration love? Don' tell me it was 'cos you wanted 'arf an hour wiv 'im discussin' ve art an' craft a' learnin' 'ow ter lift shovels or wotevver 'e's at.

Leaning down to his prick.

Greetin's. Ow are you this mornin'? O.K. are yer? This is Sharon 'ere. Come ter pay my respects. Sharon. You mus' know me? I'm ver one oose ol' lady cleans dahn yore office? Remember? I come in yore garage on Brixton 'Ill an' arst you if you would chrain a school leaver wiv no qualifications ter be a mechanic. Surely yoo remember? You said 'Woss 'is name love?' An 'I said 'Sharon.' An' you said 'Funny name fer a bloke' an' I said 'Why donch yoo go an' wrap yore prick rahnd a fan belt an' make sure iss movin?' An' you looked quite surprised. Yoo din't know wot you'd said wrong didjer? Well I jus' wan' ed ter know 'ow you do it. 'Ow you manage ter go up an' dahn an' rahnd abaht an' in an' out a' chrousers an' up the mos' respectable people an' inter restaurants and on the Cross Channel Ferry an' on the moon. I 'ear you actually set foot on the moon you was 'oppin' arahnd like a great red carrot goin' 'Vis is one step for Mankind and a big one up yours' or some such rubbish. I jus' wanner know wot is the secret a' yore success. I mean 'ow do you manage ter fit it all in John? Wot wiv the bazaars an' the lectures an' the articles in ver noospapers an' the 'it records an' the motoring offences an' jressin' up as Mrs Thatcher an' climbin' Everest 'cos it's there an' all the rest of it I mean you ain't left nuffink fer us gels 'ave yer? I mean you even do us better than we are doncher eh? Apparently you was Scout Parades wiv a coupla balloons jammed up yer more convincin' than any rotten ol' women oh an' I'll tell you this you reely know 'ow ter bring up kids. Oh you do. I mean we may do all the rubbish like carryin' 'em arahnd fer nine monfs an' wipin' their bums an' puttin' 'em ter bed an' gettin' em up buch yore the real expert aincher? Yore the one oo writes the fuckin' articles in the magazines tellin' us 'ow ter do it aincher? Yore the one oo walks in pissed at 'alf past ten an' sez 'CANCH YOO CONCHROL YORE DAUGHTER! LEAVE THIS TER ME! LEAVE THIS TER ME!' Well come on! Less av' an' answer! I 'ave never known you so fuckin' silent friend.

TRACY: Iss deaf. Don't like the light.

SUZE: Stop it. Leave off. Please. Leave off.

LINDA: Go on Derek you ain't looked yet. You might pick up a few 'ints.

CAROL: Sharon –

SHARON: Now wot we wanner know is this son. Was you the one oo landed my mate Carol in it? 'Cos yoo look remarkably similar. Abhat free inches long an' the colour a' bone meal. Like a blind worm at 'is comin' out party. Like a one-eyed, underground creature. I fink you are definitely the one responsible son an' I fink we are goin' ter 'ave ter cut you dahn ter size an' give you joo warnin' that you can't go messin' arahnd young ladies no more I fink we're goin' ter 'ave ter give you a lit'l amacher circumcision!

STEVE: Carm off it eh? A joke's a joke innit?

SHARON: A joke's a joke an' a girl's a girl an' a pair a tits is a pair a' tits an' a baby's on'y a baby so where do we go from there eh? We're gonna cut you dahn ter size son but it ain't gonna be me oo does it. Oh no. By no means. We are goin' ter use one offensive weapon on another but someone else is goin' ter carry the can. As it were. Carol!

CAROL: Sharon leave off a' me now come on less stop it less jus' leave off of it O.K? I don' wan ter do no fuckin' damage I –

SHARON: You ain't 'adjer look 'ave yer?

CAROL: Sharon I fink I reely fink. Fer Chrissake Sharon woch yoo at, yore barmy yoo are honest. Yoo reely are barmy. Blimey I –

SHARON: LOOK AT IT!

CAROL: Sharon –

SHARON: TAKE A LOOK! GO ON! TAKE A LOOK!

CAROL *turns. Looks first of all at STEVE's face and then at his prick. Initially this should be tender and at the same time threatening. She starts to shake. The violence in CAROL is suppressed and perhaps all the more frightening for that when it starts, as now, to come to the surface.*

Carol's goin' ter cut 'im.

STEVE: Carol –

CAROL: I'm a fuckin' slag I am blimey go wiv anyone. Well known. Slag or fuckin' chicken thass the choices way I see it I bloody am I tell you I bin wiv the man nex' door I bin wiv the man from the Prudential I bin wiv the milkman the baker the butcher the p'liceman the builder the dustman the windercleaner the pilot the detective the lot a' them I bin wiv everybody I'm a reel slag I'm well known fer it yoo can 'ave me fer sixpence yoo can honest.

SHARON: Walk up walk up.

CAROL: I'm fuckin' cheap I ain't got no pride I ain't a lady I ain't nuffink at all reely I tek me knickers off on Monday Choosday Wednesday Fursday Friday. Sharon don't, stop it cancher woss all this for I can't fer Gawd's sake eh? Fer Gawd's sake now –

SHARON: Take it.

CAROL *giggles. Strung out again. A hectic, dangerous sound.*

CAROL: Looks 'eavee!

SHARON: Now's your chance gel to 'ave a blow at the size nine special, the Gang Oo Couldn't Shoot Straight, the Judge in Chambers, the Law a' the Land, the P.M. the Number One Public Enemy roll up roll up grasp your weapon firmly by the 'and carm on!

CAROL *takes the bottle.*

STEVE: *Carol!*

CAROL: You shoun't reely you shoun't a' done vat woch yoo finkin' of I don't know steady on Sharon I don' mean no 'arm I ain't goin' ter 'urt no-one you shoun't though I fuckin' tell yer I'm the number one slag though 'en I aren't I owed sunnink I tell you you ain't safe I feel funny why joo do that Sharon carm on you –

STEVE: FER GAWD'S SAKE!

TRACY *is at the window with his underpants held aloft.*

TRACY: They've gone yore mates!

And almost at the same moment comes a hammering at the door and a youth's voice, that of LEROY a black youth of about STEVE's age. 'STEVE! OI! STEVE!' TRACY throws out STEVE's underpants and shuts the window. SHARON snatches the bottle from CAROL and turns to the door.

SHARON: Giss that you dozey bitch!

LEROY (*outside*): 'Ullo Steve? Steve? You vere are yer?

SHARON: Piss off lads yore mate 'opped it!

STEVE: LEROY! JOHN! I'M IN 'ERE! THEY'RE –

SHARON *turns on him. Vicious.*

SHARON: They're wot?

STEVE: Fuckin' killin' me thass all innit?

SHARON: I tell you this Stevie boy. I'd a' done you no 'arm. The one yoo wanna watch is over there.

CAROL: Sharon –

SHARON: She'd a' cut yer dahn ter size no messin'. Even ver ones wiv mascara bite an' donch yoo ferget it son. Some say they bite the fuckin' most.

SUZE: BREAK THE DOOR DOWN WE'RE ALL GOIN' TER BE MURDERED!

SHARON: WILL YOU LEAVE OFF YOU USELESS BRASS? WILL YER? YOU WAS JUST TAKEN TER PIECES DONCH YOO REMEMBER! THASS YOU ALL OVER VER FLOOR! TWENNY-ONE PHOTOGRAPHS AN' NOT A SINGLE FUCKIN' LIKENESS BECAUSE YOU DON' EXIST! YOU AIN'T THERE! YOU WAS MADE UP BY THE LIKES OF 'IM!

TRACY: Lost yer knickers now an' all.

Hammering at the door.

JOHN: Oi! You in there? Open this door up eh?

SUZE: BREAK IT DAHN! BREAK IT DAHN! BREAK IT DAHN! GO ON BREAK IT DAHN CANCHER?

SHARON: SHUT UP! SHUT UP! SHUT UP! SHUT UP!

CAROL: Stephen I'm *sorree!*

They are throwing themselves against the door outside.

SUZE: Don' nobody touch them pitchers. I'll put 'em tergevver again. I tell yer. I won' be fuckin' insulted. Worse fer fuckin' jrink yerself. Lissen. I'll put 'em tergevver again. Twenny-one likenesses indeed. I know oo *I* am thankyou madam.

Never bin so fuckin' insulted. Leave off. Leave off. Giss a lit'l peace an' quiet I arst yer. Carn a gel 'ave a quiet night. I tell yer. Leave them pitchers. I'll put 'em back up. I'll pick meself up off ver floor an' you won't know me. You won't fuckin' know me.

The door bursts back finally and LEROY and JOHN, two lads with more style and more silliness about them than STEVE but also with a genuine talent for menace, admittedly as yet undeveloped, fall into the room, acting the gangster duo for all they're worth.

JOHN: Nobody moves nobody gets hurt!

LEROY (*also mock American*): Gocher covered ladies!

JOHN: Well well well Inspector. Well well well.

Crosses to SHARON. She shows no intention of fighting.

All these birds an' on'y one real feller. Wot an opportunity eh?

SHARON: Donch yoo touch me git!

JOHN *touches her hand. Gentle at first. Then forces the broken bottle out of it, on to the floor.*

JOHN: Ah-h-h-h. In't she sweet?

Looks round.

Nah. Less 'ave a lit'l order in this establishment shall we? Shall we ladies? Woch yoo say ter that?

SHARON: Carry on lads. Thass wot we say. You 'ave a go. (*Ironical bow.*) The stage is all yours son.

Slow fade on the figures. The end of Act One.

Act Two

The same room. Just where and as we left it. JOHN *breaks into life, strutting into action. He is the leader of his particular pack, but, unlike* SHARON, *consciously exerts his authority.*

JOHN: Pour us a jrink Leroy!

SUZE: 'S over there dear.

LEROY: Thankyou Ma'am.

JOHN: Stephen if you don't mind my saying so. You look a lit'l bit of a prick.

STEVE: In't there a towel somewhere?

SUZE: There's one in –

JOHN: No towels please by order Big John. Where Steve 'as trod uvvers may foller.

TRACY: Sez yoo.

LEROY: Whiskey 'ow yoo like it Big John.

JOHN: Long an' cool an' schraight eh Leroy?

LEROY: Thass right Big Boss. Like you are.

JOHN: Kapow!

They fire imaginary guns.

LEROY: Aaaargh!

JOHN: Teach you ter mess with the Sheriff son!

STEVE: John –

JOHN: Leave it aht Stephen. You 'ave slipped up badly. You 'ave boobed. You are no longer one a' the gang. You will 'ave ter be jropped in ver river wiv concrete underpants on.

LEROY: But 'e ain't wearin' no underpants Boss!

JOHN: 'Ow intelligent you are Leroy. For a coloured person.

The two of them laugh. Posing.

SUZE: Miss 'ere as bin 'avin' a go at me aincher dearie?

SHARON: Ferget it Suze.

SUZE: Not talkin' so fuckin' big now though are yer?

SHARON: They yore kind a' people Suze are they? When in chrouble reach fer a man eh?

JOHN: Thass it darlin'. An' if yoo don' mind me sayin' so by the look a' you you reached fer a good few men in yore time.

SUZE: I beg yore pardon!

SHARON: See wot I mean?

SUZE: When I'm in chrouble gel I reach fer meself thass oo I reach for.

SHARON: Start reachin'.

TRACY: Less off Sharon.

CAROL: Yeh. I –

JOHN: STAY WHERE YOU ARE LADIES PLEASE!

Twirling his glass around.

Bleed'n'ell. We don' intend ter let vital witnesses walk out on us in vis manner. Comin' in 'ere an' findin' our mate abaht ter be turned into a fuckin' soprano by a group of sex mad young women. Oh no. We intend to investigate do we not oh black detective oo is reliable but not reely up ter bein' anyfing more than my right 'and man.

LEROY: You speak ver troof oh Caucasian sleuth.

STEVE: Less go lads an' all. I'll pick me cloves up an' –

JOHN: Yore clothes son are bein' divided between the citizens a' Chelsea. They are probably even now pinnin' labels on 'em an' sellin' 'em in Jean City son. No ladies you bin wastin' yore time wiv vis one. 'E's the runt a the litter 'e is. You should a' picked on Starsky an' me 'ere.

LINDA: All right if I make a cup a' tea Suze?

SUZE: Yes lovey.

LINDA: Carm on Derek.

DEREK: Fer fuck's sake.

LINDA: Carm along. Sugar an' milk everyone?

JOHN: Tea? Tea? We do not need tea. In ve 'ard schreets a' San Francisco we do not bovver wiv tea. We jus' stick a needle in our arms an' off we go. Two sugars. Hold the milk sweetheart.

SHARON: Sees a man an' she waits on 'im.

CAROL: Stephen I'm sorry. I wasn't –

SUZE: An' why not I'd like ter know. I mean blimey arst me ter look at meself dear buch yoo look at yoreself. Woss so wrong wiv waitin' on some man eh? I do that me own way.

SHARON: Give 'em a bit a' woch yoo do best eh?

SUZE: So wot if I do then? Well?

JOHN: 'Ello 'ello 'ello!

SUZE: None a' yore business. Well why not? Yoo know? Iss a service innit? Service is wot we're fuckin' 'ere for.

SHARON: When joo last enjoy it?

SUZE: Fer Gawd's sake! You arst me ter reach I'll fuckin' reach. I'll reach all yoo want. My first 'usband. Now wiv 'im I could 'a' made it.

JOHN: We 'ave stumbled among loose women 'ave we not oh faithful slave?

LEROY: We 'ave indeed oh Master!

STEVE: Can I 'ave sunnink ter cover me fuckin' bollocks wiv please?

JOHN: We warned you against follerin' that slag did we not? We said –

LEROY: 'These are women from anuvver galaxy!'

JOHN: 'They will steal your vital bodily essence!'

LEROY: 'They are not of our kind!'

JOHN: 'They are Chelsea supporters!' we said.

CAROL throws STEVE a cushion.

CAROL: There y'are Stephen!

JOHN: Oooh!

SHARON: She's kissin' an' makin' up Stevie boy. But she still got 'er teef aincher Carol?

CAROL: Leave me alone Sharon. I'm goin' ter do wot I wanner do fer a change O.K? If I wanner talk to 'im I'll talk to 'im O.K? Whenever I like O.K?

JOHN: An' us love?

CAROL: Yore nuffink ter me yoo are. I seen yore sort before. Yore jus' a lit'l boy far as I'm concerned.

LINDA: Lovelee innit Derek. One a' them electric ovens.

DEREK: Lissen Linda I'm still at fuckin' school I am I carn' afford no electric oven.

JOHN: Funny fing is young lady. That you are the on'y one a' the 'ole bunch oo done anyfing at all fer me an' Leroy 'ere ain't that right Leroy.

LEROY: Thass right Big Bawss. (To CAROL.) You are the Chief's woman.

SHARON: That leaves you an' me dunnit

Sambo.

LEROY: Piss off Gorgonzola.

SUZE: In *fact*. If you mus' know. My firs' 'usband was in fact a photographer. An' my Gawd I 'ad a good time wiv 'im I bloody well did. I never stopped I tell yer an' if you *mus'* know 'e done them pitchers there *an'* a' the kids!

JOHN: Wot is this woman on abaht.

SHARON: She is reviewin' 'er past life. Under guidance from Sharon 'ere.

TRACY: She's goin' ter repent of 'er wicked ways incher Suze? An' take up workin' in a shop again.

SUZE *is crossing to the pictures of herself scattered on the floor.*

JOHN: Does she regret 'er lifetime of bein' a prostitute?

SUZE: Oh piss off sonny. 'Ow come every girl i'nt a tart eh?

CAROL: Was that the one oo took them pitchers Suze? Yore first 'usband?

SUZE: Thass it. Look at this one. I look reely mean in this one. Oh blimey an' 'ere wot *am* I doin' 'ere eh?

SHARON: Keep reachin' Suze.

SUZE: I 'ad me 'air done special fer that. An' fer *that* . . .

Absorbed in the images of herself she sits among them. LINDA *and* DEREK *are making the tea with much bossing from* LINDA . . . *'Two sugars schoopid. Stop moanin' cancher? I dunno where was you jragged up I'd like ter know.'* JOHN *and* LEROY *aren't that interested in* SUZE.

JOHN: No my dear young lady –

TRACY: Thass Carol thass Sharon I'm Tracy thass Linda an' Derek an' she's Suze an' iss 'er flat.

JOHN: Carol. Young Stephen was the wrong man. 'E 'as not winnin' ways. Nah women it is well known Leroy like yoo to be definite.

LEROY: You are the boss, Boss.

JOHN: Becos women are not definite. They are all lovely and vague and confused an' schoopid an' wet an' brainless int' they? (*Close to* CAROL.) An' they wear beautiful soft garments an' 'ave Badedas barves ter make 'em smell nice an' they pour unguents over theirselves an' caper abaht in lace undies dishin' aht Cornflakes ter the two men in their lives an' oh Christ they are lovely are women giss a Kleenex 'Erbert!

LEROY: 'Ave you come Oh Mightier than the Giant Thing of the Planet Theng?

JOHN: Later young coloured person. In my own good time. Hold on to your spermatozoa. That is a trick I learned in Alcatraz.

SHARON: You one a' them junior villains are yer?

JOHN: I 'ave bin in the odd nick.

He strides about part jokey, part for real.

I was in a Junior Neighbour'ood Just up the Road Ring Twice and Ask For Arthur Remand and Improvement Short Stay Young Offenders 'Oliday Camp. On'y they closed it dahn on account they ran aht a' money. Then I was in a Maximum Security Intensive Care Ferapy Very Dangerous Young Loonies Zoo an' Rotunda. But that could not 'old me.

LEROY: Wiv one bound you was free.

JOHN: Cryin' 'My Probation Officer owes me money!'

LEROY: You are a violent man Starsky.

JOHN: I am I am.

STEVE: Violent nuffink yore all talk nah leave off slobberin' over Carol cancher?

JOHN: 'Carol' eh? Yo ho ho. A knight errant I do declare.

CAROL: I dunno woch yore on abaht Mr Big Man I reely don't I've never *seen* such a *performance* in my *life* if you wanna know an' I've never been so *embarrassed* if you must know so *there*.

JOHN: You see? I am well in there. Now dance fer us young lady. Dance.

CAROL: Piss off!

JOHN: We are going ter have ter play this one mos' carefully oh Impeccable Manservant an' incredibly good long jumper.

LEROY: Too right White Knight.

SUZE has been sorting through the pictures. She turns to SHARON.

SUZE: Nah you say fuckin' reach thass all very well I tell you I did enjoy it I did. 'E was very nice ter me was Paul. We wen' aht we wen' jrinkin' we went dancin' I was reely livin' when I was wiv 'im I tell you that.

JOHN: A fruitcake oh Black Jack.

LEROY: A bananas tart mighty whitey!

SUZE (*to SHARON*): But why joo 'ave ter come eh? I mean why joo 'ave ter start on me like that? 'Cos now yoo 'ave 'aven't you an' I dunno I look at ver fuckin' things an' I can't remember an' wot I can remember tells me it wasn't fuckin' worf it. Paul was off quick enough when I started ter slip I tell yer. 'E took the fuckin' money an' ran didn't 'e? An' 'e never cared for Jerry the way 'e should –

SHARON: Keep on reachin'.

SUZE: You reckon I'm nuffink doncher? You 'ave no opinion a' me well I got an opinion a' myself I don' care if I never fuckin' sorted why should I like it iss none a' yore business whevver I liked it or not I dunno wot it adds up to thass my affair innit fer Chrissake eh? Women this an' women that yore against women yoo are aincher?

SHARON: Lissen Suze I got no quarrel wiv you. Like you said you sort yerself.

SUZE: Easier said than fuckin' done innit? (*Dropping the photographs through her hands.*) No I never did wanna know. I wanna know though. Wot? Thass wot I wanna know. Wot an' why an' wherefore an' Gawd knows wot else Jesus Paul went when Jerry was two, David went when Tommy come on Christ all I 'ad was boys if they'd stayed I'd a – (*Crumbling a picture of herself.*) Ah they was took I wasn't a fit muvver.

JOHN: Dance Carol dance.

LINDA and DEREK are handing round the tea . . .

CAROL: No I fuckin' won't. Not fer you.

SHARON: See?

JOHN: Oh carm along gel you will dance. I mean – jus' ter look ach yer yore a walkin' invitation ter rape aincher? Everyfing abaht yer is jus' designed ter make a man ferget 'isself innit? 'Ow could you blame any red-blooded male for whipping off 'is chrousers an' runnin' at yer like 'is life depended on it. No jury would convict.

STEVE: Leave off of 'er.

SHARON: A *protector*!

STEVE: An' stop comin' on yore some kind a' juvenile delinquent yore a fuckin' apprentice you are. You foller yore ol' man arahnd wiv a bucket an' spade.

TRACY: Beach attendant are yer?

JOHN: My ol' man is a plasterer slag an' donch yoo ferget it. 'E's the bes' fuckin' plasterer in Souf London 'e is. Nobody slaps on a bag a' Carlite bondin' like my ol' man. 'E used ter do it when it was all lime an' 'air an' all reel skilful mouldin's my Gawd my ol' man's a craftsman 'e is none a' yore in an' aht jobs. Donch yoo knock my Dad slag. An' I may be 'is apprentice by day but by night I am a man a' the schreets I am a fuckin' twentief cenchry werewolf I am am I not oh dusky raver?

LEROY: You are ve 'onky 'oo cannot go wonky, Squire.

STEVE: Dance fer me then Carol.

CAROL: Oh gech yoo.

SHARON: Really is boys only innit. The men fight it out. 'Ow fuckin' pafetic.

JOHN: I goch yore number Butch Cassidy. You wanna be a man you do. Thass why yore wavin' a broken bottle rahnd my mate's equipment innit? Well I'm sorry darlin' you cannot be a man. That offer closed on November the twenty-ninf.

SHARON: I wouldn't be a man if you paid my rent fer fuckin' life.

LEROY: Everyone wants ter be a man slag. This is nach'ral.

CAROL: O.K. I'll dance. Stephen.

JOHN: Oh ho.

CAROL: Shuch yer face. Gess a record on Chrace!

TRACY: Vere's one 'ere called 'Rave On'.

SUZE: Oh thass lovely that is. I used ter play that 'fore I met Paul. When I wuz practically a virgin. When I was livin' wiv my muvver in 'Ornsey. Blimey. Meetin' you lot brings all that back. Oh I was much admired then I was. I was fuckin' sought after.

SHARON: Less go Carol.

CAROL: *No*!

SHARON: O.K. you do as you like buch yoo don' go blamin' me O.K? Don' go blamin' men when fings gets rough 'cos they fuckin' will yer know these lads ain't messin' abaht I'm afraid ter say.

CAROL: Put it on Chrace!

TRACY: Will do.

SUZE (*to* SHARON): Wot I don' get abaht yoo is you start sunnink buch yoo can't finish. I don' reckon yore interested you know wot? I reckon yore one a' them destructive types. I – (*Tearing one up. She rises.*) I'll show yoo gel I go a long way back I can reach. I amount ter sunnink I'll thank yoo ter remember O.K?

SHARON: Keep reachin'.

The music starts. SUZE *rises unsteadily and wobbles her way back to a cupboard backstage.* TRACY *stands guard by the music centre as* CAROL, *with many flirty glances to* STEVE, *takes the floor, watched by the rest of them.*

Blimey Carol wonch yoo ever learn eh?

CAROL: Nice an' loud Trace. Nah watch vis Stephen.

JOHN: *Stephen!*

LEROY: She 'as obviously fallen for your weakest servant O Timelord.

CAROL *starts to dance, enjoying it, especially as far as it is for* STEVE . . .

JOHN: But like your people Leroy she is a beautiful mover.

LEROY: She 'as nach'ral grace an' rhythm Bawss.

SUZE: Where the fuck did I put 'em?

She's ransacking drawers.

SHARON: Gettin' off on this are yer Stevey boy? Good as yer maggies is it?

JOHN: Never mind our weaker brovver slag. *I* am becomin' excited.

LEROY: Are yore pulses quickenin' Batman?

JOHN: I fink I am turnin' inter ve Incredible 'Ulk.

STEVE: Go it Carol!

JOHN: Gecher blouse off then!

CAROL: Do you mind?

STEVE: Yeh. Go on. Get 'em off eh?

SHARON: Satisfied are yer?

STEVE: Carm on Carol!

CAROL: Look at me go!

Getting off on herself. She starts to strip her blouse off. Very slow. Almost, you might say, professional.

SHARON: Fer fuck' sake Carol! Leave it aht cancher? Woch yoo chryin' ter do? Ah carm on. Don' play this one willyer? Blimey you –

CAROL: Woss got inter you?

SHARON: I'll tell yer woss got inter me. A lot a' things got inter me. My Dad comin' in an' beltin' my ol' lady thass got inter me! An' some gel I saw dahn Piccadilly I can't remember when wiv 'er face in a sling and needles up 'er arm goin' up ter blokes an' sayin' 'fancy a bit?' an' (*Indicating* SUZE *who is rooting in cupboards at the back.*) 'er if you wanna know 'er an' all thass got inter me an' all fuckin' women who act up to it an' fawn an' cringe an' beg fer it an' then bite their fuckin' knuckles wiv rage 'cos vey're nuffing an' they got nuffing 'part from veir tits that they sling an' their knickers they bought on the 'ire purchase an' they ain't got no pride no nuffink wot makes a woman a woman I tell you oh fer Chrissake Carol *stop it*!

CAROL: Ooo's beggin' nah then eh? 'Oo's beggin' nah eh? 'Ere we go Stephen, 'ere we go then . . .

JOHN: Less 'ave a look –

SHARON: An' don' run away wiv the notion you can do that fer one man an' one alone. Oh no. You joined the fuckin' club Carol you joined the fuckin' club!

JOHN: Go it Carol!

CAROL (*as she slips her blouse off*): An' when I finished doin' it wiv the milkman an' the baker an' the candlestick maker an' the man from the Insurance and the ice cream man an' the Prime Minister I don it wiv a candle an' a telephone an' a broomstick an' a glass jar an' an aubergine an' a length a rubber an' a telephone directory an' my uncle an' I

took the pill an' I 'ad an abortion an' I fitted a cap an' I tried on a coil an' I –

SHARON: STOP IT!

CAROL *giggling hysterically, throws away her blouse and sits next to* STEPHEN. *Kissing him casually.*

CAROL: Oooh look at me!

LEROY: I 'ave the strange female garment oh pale male.

SHARON *moves towards him.*

JOHN: Avoid our strange friend from the planet Ugly young coloured person.

LEROY: I go I go.

LEROY *skips away towards the window.*

JOHN: Doubtless in 'er attempts ter be a man she 'as bin injectin' 'erself wiv 'ormones like them Russian afletes an' spendin' nights at the Y.M.C.A. in order ter find aht 'ow iss done.

BOTH: 'Y.M.C.A.!'

CAROL *goes back to* STEPHEN.

CAROL: I'll sit wiv 'im if thass O.K? (*A giggle as she sits on the arm of his chair.*) Nudist corner.

JOHN: A – ah woch yoo goin' ter do nah Stevie boy eh? Move that cushion are yer? Eh?

But CAROL *and* STEVE *look quite matey. This irks both* SHARON *and* JOHN *for different reasons. Back of the room* SUZE *has found some letters through which she is sorting.* TRACY *pockets cassettes while* DEREK *and* LINDA *watch . . .*

LINDA: We'll wash up them cups next.

DEREK: Oh will we then?

LINDA: Yes. We will.

CAROL: Where was we Stephen?

STEVE: You was tellin' me you lived on an estate. An' I adn't tolj yoo I live on an estate an' all.

CAROL: Oh frills eh?

STEVE: Brilliant. Woch yoo do Carol?

CAROL: I work in a jry cleaners. So does Chrace. So does Sharon. *Sort of.*

JOHN: This is worse that fuckin' useless

Stephen. You ain't touched 'er yet. You ain' even goch yore arm rahnd 'er.

LEROY *is at the window.*

While the lady of yore choice is forced ter watch 'er blouse mingle wiv yore underpants many floors below.

And her blouse has gone.

CAROL: That was *noo.* Mister.

JOHN: Maybe.

CAROL: Yore a pig you are.

JOHN: I am. I am one a' them male chauvinist pigs woch yoo read abaht. I believe that as far as women is concerned you should schrike first an' ask questions afterwards. As far as I am concerned women is like flesh and blood Monopoly.

SHARON: Which is wot 'is fuckin' mate finks on'y 'e ain't got the guts ter say it Carol.

JOHN: Women, women, young slaggy person is the plaything of an idle hour. They are a leisure activity. They should be kept under a tight rein. They should be saddled and bridled and muffled and hobbled an' generally made abaht as safe as Fort Knox an' allowed out ter Lipton's once a fortnight in order ter give 'em a lit'l lift is not this so my tinted friend?

LEROY: Even among us ignorant black people oh cream dream we make sure that our women is soldered to the back kitchen wall.

JOHN *is standing by* CAROL.

JOHN: Thass a real woman for you Imitation Man. Lovely breasts peepin' aht like lit'l rabbits.

SUZE: Steady *on!*

SHARON: Ah ha. Signs a' life!

JOHN: Delicately made lit'l shoulders. Neck there. Neck. Best end a' neck. An' buddin' up in ver middle there like Spring in Appalachia like a peach sundae alone in ver fridge like dawn in the fuckin' Pyrenees there there are the lower slopes of the slag ooo is wastin' 'er time wiv the Gang Wanker. Oh whipped cream! Oh whipped cream! Oh lovely fuckin' grub. Grab a spoon you shade in the spade.

LEROY: Kirk ter ship Kirk ter ship. My ray gun is stuck up my own arse!

SUZE: Leave off of'er!

SHARON: More like it.

JOHN: Shuch yer face brass!

SUZE: Donch yoo brass me sonny.

SHARON: Nice!

JOHN: Shut up the two a' yer!

SHARON: Don't let the advance guard fool yer Suze. They come in fuckin' droves an' they fight between theirselves like fuckin' dogs. Yap yap yap over a bleed'n bone donch yoo be fooled. Man I might give yer once every ten years but men oh no no bleed'n way.

SUZE: I jus' found this letter from my ol' lady. (*Laughing hopelessly.*) Oh Jesus maybe yore right maybe you are. I'm a dumb bloody slag I am 'en I when all's said an' done. (*Reads:*)
Dear Suze,
How are you both?

Looks up.

Bitch. (*Reads:*) '. . . I am so looking forward to the wedding. Paul will –' (*But she's laughing too much to go on.*) Oh I dunno I reely don't.

STEVE (*to* SHARON): You two are makin' aht incher?

SHARON: We are makin' progress.

SUZE: Oh don't say that love. I'll never make progress. Don' start me on that caper. You set me finkin' thas all. I do plenty a' that in my own time I do assure you. But I tell you it all comes back ter the kids.

TRACY: Oh ta!

SUZE: See if Paul'd stayed . . . I mean iss tough on yore own see wot I mean? I mean they 'ave 'em wiv yer don't they?

JOHN: Ark at 'er!

SUZE: Oh fuck off! (*Coming back to the group.*) Look it makes an 'ome dunnit? I mean after Paul I always thought . . .

LINDA: You get an 'ome when yore married.

SHARON: She's always on abaht an' 'ome. Donch yoo start 'er off. (*Switching from* SUZE *to* LINDA, *the brief possibility of rapport broken.*) Yeh, an' iss got a sink that don't work an' two kids an' you can't pay the gas bills an' yoo 'ave ter live in it an' all while 'e's off at the bleed'n pub doncher?

SUZE: I carn explain ter you gels can I? Can't jus make you see.

Holding their attention.

There must a bin a reason why I chried it again and again. I seen ver same fing 'appenin' but I chried. An' wot was weird after I 'ad Jerry I never enjoyed it. Blimey 'alf a London'd bin lookin' up my snatch. Doctors'd shone lights up it midwives'd stuck probes up it fuckin' Jerry 'ad battered it for abaht eighteen hours I tell you I was practically runnin' fuckin' guided tours. As fer it bein' *mine.* No chance it was the bleed'n M.1. It was runway free at London Airport. (*To* SHARON:) But I chried din't I? I kept on chryin'. 'Cos arter Paul there was David and there was Tommy blimey I coun't tell the difference between the ones oo were chryin' ter get up me an' the ones oo was chryin' ter get out but I kept on chryin' eh? Now why? Why?

SHARON: 'Cos yore schoopid.

SUZE: Lissen – (*Gentle to* SHARON. JOHN *doesn't like it.*)

JOHN: Slag will ter slag my friend. Eventually. O loose bleed'n woman.

SUZE (*hard to him*): Yore a performer you are.

JOHN (*posing*): But wot abaht the rest of our young friend eh lads? This is on'y the horses' doovers innit? This is wotcher might call the appetiser ter set yore average young stallion 'itchin' up 'is leg an' initiatin' a spine shatterin' fuck.

CAROL: You'll be lucky mate.

LINDA: More tea anyone? Vere's a lot in the pot.

SUZE: 'Ta lovey.

LINDA: Carm on Derek giss a 'and!

STEVE: I fink iss time you took sunnink else off though. Actually. I mean iss on'y fair innit? I mean I got my gear off didn't I?

CAROL: Well iss different fer you innit?

STEVE: Why is it?

SHARON: Becos in case you 'adn't noticed 'Erbert men wiv no cloves don' run ver risk a' bein' –

JOHN: Raped.

SHARON: Thankyou.

A nasty moment.

STEVE: Ah carm on oo's talkin' abaht rape.

JOHN: We are sellotape features. Me an' the 'uman gumboil 'ere are talkin' abaht rape. Me an' Spacewoman Perkins are discussin' the seizin' of lovely young white limbs an' the pantin' an' groanin' an' slobberin' as the 'orrible 'airy legged young waiter from Balham oose mind 'as bin turned by lookin' at adverts fer Pretty Polly tights penetrates the innermost recesses of the young lady of 'is choice.

CAROL: Yore creepy you are.

STEVE: Off they come then!

And he grabs at her jeans. The two struggle, giggling on the floor, and finally he gets them over her knees. LEROY *and* JOHN *join in at the end,* LEROY *walking away with her jeans.*

SUZE: This'll end in tears I tell yer.

SHARON: An' 'ow did it fuckin' start I'd like ter know.

CAROL: STEPHEN!

STEVE: 'OORAY!

JOHN: Touchin' innit?

LEROY: 'E is doin' no more than warmin' 'er up fer you oh mightier than Bionic Brian the Fulham Striker. I 'ave not 'ad a white woman since I was on de plantation.

JOHN: AN' SHE'S WEARIN' FUCKIN' TIGHTS!

STEVE: Get out of it!

JOHN: She is though in't she? She is wearin' fuckin' tights. I mean wot a carry on. Wot a bleed'n cop out eh? This is it wiv girls though innit? Wot they promise they never deliver.

CAROL: Watch woch yore doin' wiv them jeans.

LEROY: We will!

JOHN: All tease. All tease. Take off a bit flash it abaht an' underneaf she's got 'er bum in a fuckin' schring bag in't she? Oh it is so fuckin' confusin' though innit? Like every time you wen' in the butcher's there was this lamb chop sidles up ter yer an' said 'Fancy a bit do yer?' but 'fore you could pop it in very schring bag it 'ad scuttled back ter ver fridge. Teasers. Look at that. Blimey if I bin let dahn by one fing in my life iss bleed'n women's underwear innit? You see it in the telly an' iss floatin' arahnd an' silky an' comes ter bits in yer 'and an' then you get up against some slag after the pubs shut an' woch yoo got. Oh most horrible my friends. You got handkerchief pie. You got soiled linen. You got birds wiv veir fuckin' bums in schring bags. A con a most decided con.

Pause.

I used ter foller this bird dahn our schreet. I mean jus' ter look at 'er know wot I mean? An' I used ter watch 'er go in 'er 'ouse 'an I used ter know when she was goin' upstairs an' me an' my mate used ter watch 'er you know, gettin' ready fer bed an' that. An' oh blimey. Wot an anticipation. Over the shoulders. Bra off. Corsets. She wore fuckin' corsets. She must a' bin abaht fifty an' out it came like the bleed'n Aswan Dam tits inter stomach inter –

Stops himself before it gets heavy.

STEVE: Lissen to 'im eh?

SHARON: You got one very sick boy there Stephen.

SUZE: Now lissen ter me. I'll say it to yer. I'll say it to yer.

Trying to cool it. But JOHN *jaunts up to* CAROL.

JOHN: Less 'ave the bra off.

CAROL: No.

SHARON *gets up. Perhaps alarmed by* JOHN *suddenly.*

JOHN: Easy Batwoman. My African manservant 'as goch you well covered. 'E is chrained in the Eastern arts a' self defence including Kung Fu Karate Sumo Wrestlin' an' leapin' out at people from be'ind black plastic bags wiv lengfs a lead pipin'. In short let us keep this peaceful.

CAROL: Well I ain' goin' ter take my bra off an' thass final. Thass completely final

an' definite that is innit Sharon?

SHARON: You started it.

CAROL: Started wot I'd like ter know.

SHARON: You an' yore fuckin' friend. Amuse 'im amuse the lot.

CAROL: Give over.

TRACY: You took yore bra off in that shed dincher?

STEVE: I know wot we'll 'ave the tights.

CAROL: Give over!

But for STEVE *it is a girlish shriek and she is still laughing as he wrests her out of them. Unseen by her* LEROY *goes to the window with her trousers.* JOHN *is implacably watching, the violence in him more evident now.*

Well thass the lot. Blimey. On'y got me undies left 'en I?

SHARON: Oh that was always the fuckin' lot wasn't it Carol. An' when fings got rough you bleed'n cried ter me well fer Gawd's sake donch yoo see yerself Carol? You make a fuckin' spectacle of yourself you do woch yoo wanna be like them magazine women is it all flash this an' flash that fer 'Eaven's *sake.*

CAROL: Ah leave off me Sharon. I wanner be me if you wanner know an' woss so wrong wiv vat. An' if you mus' know I like wearin' nice clothes an' I like the way boys look at me when I go down the schreet an' I like ter look sexy an' I like lipstick an' showin' meself off an' all that I enjoy it. O.K? Thass wot I call livin' if you mus' know. An' I dunno 'ow long I'll be livin' 'fore I'm sick like yore ol' lady 'angin' rahnd ver launjrette an' waitin' up fer yore ol' man an' 'avin' Gawd knows 'ow many kinds 'angin' rahnd me an' 'Mummy this' and 'Mummy that' my Gawd if you mus' know Sharon all my life all I fuckin' wanner do is shine up there like a dancer or sunnink. Like sunnink reely glamorous that everyone wants an' I can't see woss so wrong wiv vat. 'Cos I ain't gonner get no kitchen wiv pitcher winders an' some geezer wiv a pipe like you was on abaht am I now? I be lucky I get any bloke fer more'n two monfs togevver like *my* ol' lady I suppose an' if I get a bloke 'e'll be aht a' work or 'e'll set me ter the bleed'n game like *'er* I wouldn't be surprised but if you reely want ter know jus' fer now for this minute I wanner enjoy it. I wanner go up in a pile a' smoke an' flames an' eye shadder an' levver shoes an' dancin' an' all that I'll go like them girls in the magazines Sharon an' you ain't goin' ter stop me. O.K?

JOHN: Bra off.

CAROL: SHUCH YORE FACE CREEP!

JOHN: OFF OR YORE IN CHROUBLE GEL!

STEVE: Steady John. Nuffink 'eavy eh?

CAROL *de-escalates it.*

CAROL: They're dear anyway are brassieres.

STEVE: If she don't want to leave 'er.

He makes a grab for her bra. She giggles and backs away. Sees LEROY *who drops her trousers out of the window with a malicious smile.*

CAROL: YOU MEAN BLACK BASTARD!

JOHN: Look Miss. You are takin' off yore fuckin' bra whevver you like it or not an' it ain't nuffink ter do wiv 'ow many cloves young Loopy 'ere took off this is a question a' me an' Leroy gettin' a gander ach yore Bristols so if you *won't* take 'em off me an' Leroy is goin' ter 'ave ter take 'em off for yer.

STEVE: No need ter be so fuckin' 'eavy John I tell yer iss on'y –

JOHN: Oh you was well in there when we arrived werencher? You was in the buff you was. Def'nitely in conchrol a' the situation. No wonder she likes you boy yore putty in 'er 'ands you are.

SHARON: An' it's s'posed ter be ve ovver way arahnd innit?

SUZE: I dunno any more. When I look at the bollocks I made a' my life I tell yer I don' know.

She sits by the photos and adds her pile of letters to them. At some point in the following dialogue she goes back to the room and collects other trinkets, letters, pictures etc. Sorting through them as if she was ready to clean up the place.

You see I look at you lot you could be my bleed'n children couldn't yer? I mean lookin' ach yoo lot I wonder wot my kids

are doin'? I dunno. Jumpin' up an' dahn on some old lady. In some nick or uvver. Jrinkin' too much. Wearin' safety pins in their ears. 'Avin' a number one 'aircut an' schrugglin' inter their first pair a Doctor Martins, nickin' bikes. You see all the things I wan'ed ter tell 'em. Oh I wan'ed ter tell im 'ow it was. 'Ow ter do it. An' now I'm tellin' yoo an' yoo lot pay me no more attention. Buch yoo gotter listen.

SHARON: Well woch yoo sayin'?

SUZE: I'm sayin' yore young thass all. An' I'm sayin' it ain't that simple. And when you got ter where I am yoo'll understand. Buch yore like lit'l animals. I dunno woch yore livin' off. I wan' a tell yoo. I wanner say –

SHARON: WHAT THOUGH EH? WOT?

JOHN: Now you slag. Fer the lars' time of askin' off wiv that bra a' yores. That is an order.

CAROL: NO!

JOHN: O.K.!

And he and LEROY *fall on her.* STEVE *joins in but although he tries to fight them off it's still of the order of a playground scuffle rather than anything nastier. Eventualy* JOHN *breaks away with the bra in his hand.* CAROL, *in spite of her anger at* JOHN, *is laughing, pleased to be the centre of attention.*

JOHN: Does it suit me?

LEROY: A wondrous sight O Elder of the Night.

JOHN: Never before 'ave these garments reached our planet. Yore civilisation mus' be years a head of ours O woman.

SHARON: It is you greasy lit'l wanker.

JOHN: Ouch!

LEROY: Kapow!

CAROL: Well there. Now you seen 'em.

STEVE (*sincere*): They're great Carol. They're lovely tits. Honest.

CAROL: You reckon?

STEVE: Yeh. Honest. Reely firm.

JOHN: Ahhhh. 'E likes 'em. 'E finks vey're lovely. (*Up to her again.*) 'Ere they are lads. The two big ones. Roll up roll up.

Muvver's special. None a' yore Brazilian tribeswoman lark oh no these are wot I would call breasts. Notice the lit'l red fings on ver front. These are known as nipples. Ring for service. Look at 'em. (*Going behind her.*) We are now passing above the cleavage which can be seen below us on the right. If any passenger leans out he may fall in an' I mus' warn you that lads oo fall dahn the cleavage never can recover. Surely there is nuffink lovelier than a woman's breasts. I know some people say 'What is the point a' them two bags a skin bumpin' arahnd an' gettin' in the way?' I know there are those oo are of ve opinion that all this strokin' 'em an' bitin' 'em is a big waste a' time but not me. I do not agree wiv vose oo declare that they resemble warts or boils or – (*Stops himself before the hatred shows.*) Shake 'em about a bit love. This is wot it is all abaht innit?

SHARON: Rarver shack up wiv a feller wouj yer Johnnie?

JOHN: An' they speak too don't they? Thass wot I can't stand abaht women. As well as all . . . this . . . they come equipped wiv' voices. 'Jus' do this love!' 'Don't be late!' ''Ow do I look?' Orderin' yer lyin' to yer messin' you up. Blimey. Abaht as much fun as a game at Millwall. On'y fing ter do wiv girls is go in there in an armoured car pick out the girl you wan, fuck 'er, bash 'er on the 'ead an' then off dahn to the pub fer a few needful pints a lager. Deep deep down they wanner do the same ter you. Or worse, fuckin' marry you.

LINDA: Nuffink wrong wiv marriage. Marriage is nach'ral. I'm goin' ter get married.

JOHN: See wot I mean? From the cradle they are dangerous.

STEVE: Wot makes you the expert on gels all of a sudden John?

JOHN: Lissen –

STEVE: I wasn't aware you was such an expert.

JOHN: Oh wasn't you?

STEVE: I was not.

TRACY: 'Ow does it feel Carol to 'ave all these geezers fightin' over you.

CAROL: Thrilling I'm sure.

JOHN: I know plenty abaht girls. I know they 'ang arahnd in corners whisperin' abaht eye shadder. I know 'ow they like it. Uvver week I'm in a pub 'en I? an' iss gel . . . she's givin' me the eye in't she? Oglin'.

LEROY: Winkin' oh Man a' the Moment.

JOHN: Winkin' as it might be. So I goes over to 'er. 'Ullo!' I sez – 'woss your name then?' 'Rita!' she sez. 'Right Rita!' I sez ''ow about a fuck?' 'Fair enough!' she sez, 'fair enough.' Out we go to 'er car. Now I've 'ad it in every kind a car. I've 'ad women in every fuckin' make a' car there is. I even done it in a Deux Chevaux. For a bet. Anyway. This bird drives a fuckin' Volvo don't she? Bleed'n great fing. A fully automated up'olstered maroon two point sunnink or ovver Volvo. 'Right!' sez Rita, 'take it away!' So I gets inter the car an' we take it away. She takes off her bra –

LEROY: Slowly.

JOHN: While I put the ol' engine inter neutral an' take off the 'andbrake. An' 'en she eases aht of 'er jress an' shimmies out of 'er knickers.

LEROY: While you switch on the ignition.

JOHN: I do Leroy. I am no fool. Taking care not ter give it too much choke. So that the engine does not flood with what is gen'rally known as rich mixture.

LEROY: None richer.

JOHN: An' nah she is naked. Gleamin' white on the fuckin' dashboard in't she? She's got 'er fuckin' thigh over the speedo an' 'er tits up by the stick shaft which is situated on ver steering column.

SHARON: You know yore way arahnd cars then son doncher?

JOHN: I place my 'and on 'er knee an' the engine leaps inter life. We are careerin' arahnd this car park. ''Ello 'ello' she sez, 'you ain't turned my fuckin' lights on!' 'Yore lights!' I sez 'Oh Christ yore lights' I put 'em on 'Sidelights only!' she sez 'carm on carm on' 'Dipped headlights lady' I sez she sez 'Main beam Maim beam!' we're on main beam I sez '*Move* up ver fuckin' gears' she sez 'Double de-clutch!' I sez 'Second inter third!' She sez 'CHANGE UP CHANGE UP I'M FUCKIN' READY FOR IT FER GAWD'S SAKE

CHANGE UP!' I SEZ "ANG ON I'M
COMIN' I'M COMIN'" SHE SEZ
'WAIT FER ME FER FUCK'S SAKE
WAIT FER ME!' I SAY 'FORTY
FIFTY SIXTY SEVENTY' 'YES! YES
YES!' SHE SEZ 'YES! YES! YES!' AN'
WE'RE DOIN' EIGHTY NINETY
ONE FUCKIN' UNJRED MILES AN
HOUR WE ARE DOIN' THE TON
AN' WE ARE FUCKIN' MAKIN' IT IT
IS AMAZIN' IT IS INCREDIBLE IT IS
SO BLEED'N *GOOD*!!!

LEROY: An' then you realise.

JOHN: No petrol.

LEROY: Police arrive.

JOHN: Mop you up.

LEROY: Two years.

JOHN: Wot a waste a' fuckin' time. (*He's now up by* CAROL.) No. I'm sunnink of an expert on gels an' women. Fast cars fast women an' long cool glasses a' Bacardi thass me.

CAROL: Jigsaw puzzles an' digestive biscuits mate thass you. Blimey.

JOHN: The insolence of this woman! (*Touching her leg.*) Leg eh? Leg. Donch yoo love women's legs. All soft an' lovely. Like a boiled piece a' chicken. Ideal fer openin'. Lovely fer layin' yore 'ead on while she sorts frough yore 'air fer lice or nits. 'Hullo Doris! When are we ter be married?'

LINDA: Yoo got a reel down on marriage aincher? Carm on Derek less tidy up then.

DEREK: No.

LINDA: *Derek*!

DEREK: Less off shall we?

LINDA: One more fer the road eh?

DEREK: You really can fuckin' jrink cancher?

JOHN: Women's bums. Gordon Bennet I love women's bums. Don' I Leroy?

LEROY: You do rude dude!

JOHN: Sometimes I fink women's bums are the absolute star attraction. I mean there too good ter sit dahn on reely in't they? When yore depressed, when yore seasick when yore reely in the fuckin' dumps, when yore team lost an' you gotter start at

five o'clock nex' mornin' ter get ter some fuckin' site in Barnet or bleed'n Enfield or some place the ovver side a' the world you turn over in bed and you twist yore pajama schrings rahnd yore finger an' yoo' 'fink 'Well son. Women's bums.' Thass woch yoo fink. 'Arses' you fink quietly ter yoreself 'Buttocks' 'Rears' 'Posteriors' 'Be'inds' 'Bottoms'. Out there waitin' for yer. In chrousers in skirts in long coats grindin' tergevver, lyin' peacefully side by side, liftin' saucily up in ve air millions an' fuckin' millions of 'indquarters jus' lyin' waitin' for it wiv big sleepy grins on their faces. An' there's so much ter be done wiv a bum in't there? You can squeeze it like a lump a' pastry you can slap it you can pat it you can watch it you can tickle it or you can jus' watch it gettin' on wiv its daily round under the petticoat of the lady of yore choice, like two kids fightin' under a blanket, like a fuckin' windsock in a force eight gale stretchin' yearnin' dancin' away like a red rag to a bull my Gawd yes. I am a bum man an' no mistake.

CAROL: Get *off* yer rude sod!

JOHN: I am a buttock specialist, a be'ind merchant a fan a' the bottom, a fully paid up member of the arse appreciation society.

SHARON: Strike a light!

SUZE: My third was inter bums. Gawd. Bums were all 'e could fuckin' see in a woman I said to 'im I said 'I don't know why you bovver wiv me' I said 'there's more bums than women in the world an' thass a chroo fact!' Up it like a fuckin' rabbit 'e was. Terrible bloody imposition reely.

JOHN: Do you mind slag? I am chryin' out an 'ynm ter ver female body 'ere. Can we leave aht the sordid details if you please?

SUZE: Well they may be sordid details to you mate but they're our bleed'n bodies in't they?

SHARON: Go it Suze!

SUZE: This suit yer does it? (*With friendly contempt.*) Now you can *fink* woch yoo like abaht it, but at the end a' the day that is *'er* bum an' not yores O.K.? I mean you got ter 'ave a lit'l respect aincher?

TRACY: 'Course you 'ave.

SHARON: An yoo remember 'am eyes that some of us don' want no long nosed fuckin' men sniffin' rahnd our –

SUZE: NOW LEAVE THAT OUT! (*To* SHARON:) You ask me ter reach I'll reach. I 'ave standards. But donch yoo ask me ter write the 'ole lot off willyer? 'Cos I don' fancy that. Christ you do some fuckin' reachin' girl as well as 'im. Look I tell you I don't repent. Far as I'm concerned somewhere aht there is a geezer wiv bushy eyebrows an' an' 'ouse in ver counchry an' silver 'air an' ten acres a' land. An' when I meet 'im we'll jus' do it. There won't be any caperin' or arguin' or moneytalk or any a' that we'll jus' do it see? Like it was part a' 'fings. An' a' course arter a few weeks a' this 'e will propose won' e? An wot'll I do but bleed'n accept an' we'll get married in a fuckin' church wiv a fuckin' vicar an' my fuckin' Mum an' guess wot I'll wear fuckin' white I fuckin' well will I'll wear fuckin' white an' let the 'ole' wide world know that I am quite definitely one 'unjured per cent a bleed'n virgin. 'Ow about that then?

SHARON: Ah ferget it!

LINDA: I fink iss lovely.

SUZE: Good fer you Linda. You wipe them cups love. You wipe them cups.

JOHN: I fought we was talkin' abaht naked women. Some'ow or uvver the conversation 'as jrifted rahnd ter marriage.

CAROL: You was talkin' fuck-face abaht my body. Ter be precise you was talkin' abaht my be'ind. I never 'eard anyfink so schoopid in all my life well may I remind you when you all finished talkin' abaht women's body this an' women's body that it is Carol oo ain' got 'ardly a stitch on.

STEVE: An' me eh?

CAROL: I din't notice you was a woman.

STEVE: You ain't looked.

CAROL: Shuch yer face cheeky! (*Bashes him on the head with a cushion, in a basically amiable fashion.*) An' as far as I'm concerned woman's body or no woman's body I'm reasonably proud a' my tits so as far as I'm concerned the lot a' you can jus' fuck off an' if anyone ought ter be complainin' it ought ter be me but I

ain't so there so get a good look at 'em all a' yer an' then some kind soul go down four floors an' bring me bra back eh?

She gets up.

SHARON: Carol –

CAROL: Ah shut up misery. Carol this an' Carol that. Stop carryin' on at me eh?

STEVE: Gech yoo Carol!

LINDA: She's off.

TRACY: Go it Carol!

SHARON: Chrace –

TRACY: You swing 'em to the left an' you swing 'em to the right . . .

JOHN: Ease off slag!

CAROL gets up from the chair where she's been with STEPHEN and does a joke model pose, the centre of attention once more.

CAROL: Get me everybody.

She parades around the stage, literally flashing her tits at the assembled company. STEVE claps in time to her parade. There is something exuberant about it, and as a result SHARON can't quite disapprove and JOHN does not enjoy it.

SUZE: 'Ad enough 'ave yer love?

CAROL: Da di da dia da da da *da* dum dum dum di dum dum dum dum . . .

TRACY: Thass the stuff. Carol Action! Oi!

JOHN: Put 'em *away*!

STEVE: Go it Carol!

JOHN: STOP IT!

STEVE gets up, also naked, also suddenly exuberant.

STEVE (*to* SHARON): Now it can't be all bad now can it? Eh? Got ter be a bit useful. I mean it ain't the end a' the world is it if a gel wants to act up a bit. An' fer fuck's sake there's bad and good in't there? Eh? I mean you may a' fought I was full a' rubbish but blimey get a load of 'im get a load a John. Christ. I may be bad Sharon but 'e's a disaster. Never bin *near* no woman. Honest. Scared fuckin' stiff a' them. Worships 'is ol' man. Dahn the pub wiv 'em aincher John wiv 'women' this an' 'women' that but take a look at one I mean get close ter one who ain't pasted on a wall an' yoo go ter jelly doncher? So giss a break Sharon. Ease up on us eh?

JOHN: HOLD IT *THERE*!

He has picked up the broken bottle lying where it was forced from SHARON's *hands earlier. Everyone freezes.*

LEROY: Beware O Master.

JOHN: Back off Leroy.

STEVE: John –

JOHN: Now you. You wiv the tits out. You wiv the fancy to Steve the Wanker. 'Ere. Nah. O.K?

SUZE: Do wot 'e says lovey.

SHARON: You fuckin' lit'l –

STEVE: 'OLD IT! 'E'LL FUCKIN' KILL YER!

JOHN: Too right I will. (*And he does look dangerous.*) 'Fins a' bin slippin' 'ere ain't they? Slag talking ter slag an' young Stephen poncin' arahnd an' knucklin' under ter some useless bloody lesbian. 'Ere brighteyes. Over 'ere. (*Very slowly* CAROL *goes towards him. When she's quite close:*) Now I know woch yore up to. I seen yore sort before. You are strictly display goods aincher? Well you come to the wrong address becos I ain't fooled by yore act. You bin comin' that on boys fer a lit'l too long. Get 'em off.

SHARON: You bleeding animal.

JOHN: SHUCH YORE FACE!

CAROL: Yore nuffink ter me mate. You are fuck all as far as I'm concerned. Far as I'm concerned you can 'it me you can bully me you can make me take off everyfink I got yore still nuffink. Yore like those creeps I see on me way ter work whistlin' an' carryin' on well I don' mind it from some but I won't take it from a creep an' I don' care woch yoo make me do it doesn't mean a *thing*. Geddit. Now. If it'll make yore day I'll oblige. But donch yoo run away wiv the notion it means a single bleed'n *thing* far as I'm concerned.

And, full of contempt, never taking her eyes off his face, she takes off her knickers. Quite solemn, as if she was going to bed for the night, she throws her knickers to the floor and stands there, naked. In a minor key, and quietly, almost like a dirge, someone, perhaps TRACY, *is*

humming 'The Stripper.'

JOHN: Smile you slag smile.

CAROL: Fer why?

JOHN: CHEER UP A BIT CANCHER? SMILE CANCHER? IT AIN'T THE END A' THE WORLD! CARM ON LESS SEE YOU SMILE A BIT EH? MOVE IT ARAHND A BIT CARM ON STOP LOOKIN' LIKE I WAS GOIN' TER EAT YER I AIN'T GOIN' TER EAT YER SMILE FER GAWD'S SAKE SMILE!

CAROL: 'Aj yer look?

JOHN: I am warning you.

CAROL: Of wot?

He leans down to her genitals.

JOHN: 'ELLO 'ELLO! WE ARE WAITING FOR SOME SIGN OF LIFE! WE ARE WORRIED LEST YOU ARE FAST ASLEEP OR 'AVE BY CHANCE BUGGERED OFF TO SOUF AMERICA AN' LEFT A PLASTIC REPLICA OF YORESELF TER FOOL THE NEIGHBOURS!

Very close.

Wouj yoo mind tellin' us why yoo are so fuckin' cagey please? Are yoo expectin' us ter do sunnink or do we jus' 'ang arahnd waitin' fer you ter burst inter flames. Look I don' wanner be unreasonable abaht this but I find it very difficult ter carry on when I am gettin' this sort a' kickback from you. Frankly I might as well be shoutin' dahn a lift shaft or a well or the Grand Canyon all I am askin' for is a lit'l co-operation. Is that a lot to ask? Is it?

Kneeling.

We 'ave 'ad a few arguments in the past I know. There 'ave bin times when we 'ave not seen eye to eye an' I do appreciate that you are a very busy bloke wiv problems of yore own ter contend wiv but I am afraid it is not goin' ter be possible for me ter carry on like this for very much longer. If you do not mind me sayin' so it is fuckin' frustratin'.

A scream.

IT IS FUCKIN' FRUSTRATIN' CAN YOO 'EAR ME? DID JOO RECEIVE THAT MESSAGE? WIGGLE YORE

LEFT LOBE IF YOU ARE RECEIVIN' ME PLEASE! OVER AN' OUT! FER THE LARS' TIME OF ASKIN' WILL YOU STOP STANDIN' THERE DOIN' NUFFINK AN' REACH OUT TO A LAD OF SEVENTEEN YEARS OO IS GETTIN' A LIT'L BIT ON THE DESPERATE SIDE WILL YER?

Pause.

I am givin' yoo one more chance an' then I am sendin' for the police an' the Fire Brigade an' a coupla regiments a' Light Infantry an' we are comin' in after you. Do you read me Red Leader do you read me? Lissen I am well aware of your talents. I am well aware that 'arf a London 'as bin up you an' dahn you I am aware that sev'ral Russian spies took refuge inside you on'y last week I am fully up ter the fact that Organised Tours of yore extensive network of tunnels are even nah in progress I am absolutely convinced thach yoo are as exciting, mysterious, dangerous, deep, wide, long, strong, old, remarkable an' fuckin' permanent as the Cheddar Gorge or the fuckin' salt mines of Siberia. Don't worry son I'm persuaded that I myself spent a brief period of my life on this fuckin' planet kickin' arahnd in yore well up'olstered apartments. 'ELLO IS ANYONE UP THERE?

The pitch of desperation.

BUT I AM NOT AWARE REPEAT *NOT* AWARE THACH YOO ARE DOIN' ANYFING FER ME! I DO NOT SEE WHAT EARTHLY BLEED'N USE YOU ARE AS FAR AS I AM CONCERNED! AS FAR AS I AM CONCERNED ALL YOU DO IS SIT THERE GRINNIN' AN' WATCHIN' AN' WAITIN' AN' GENERALLY MESSIN' ME ABAHT! RIGHT?

CAROL: An' now you spineless git look at my face. Or donch yoo fuckin' care?

JOHN: I'LL DO MORE'N LOOK AT YORE FACE YOO SLAG!

Touching her fanny with the bottle.

STEVE: THAT DOES IT!

JOHN: Ah. Ah.

With something terribly like relief he whips round to his feet to face STEVE, who,

armed only with a cushion, is coming for him.

The 'ero of the hour. The naked monster from outer space. I wondered when yoo was gonna ride ter the rescue. Ferget it Stephen you are well aht 'a the race yoo are.

STEVE: Oh no I am not son.

SUZE: Easy!

JOHN: Fuck off brass.

As the two start to circle each other, like wolves lining up for a fight, SUZE, who has now accumulated quite a pile of jewellery, letters and pictures of herself on the floor, breaks away and follows the two boys as they circle each other across the whole area of the stage.

SUZE: I SAID 'EASY' DINCH YOO 'EAR ME? YOU MAD SODS! I'LL TELL YOU WOT I 'BIN CRYIN' TER SAY TER YOO LOT YES AN' I'LL SAY IT TO 'ER AN' ALL I'LL TELL YOU *NUFFINK* AIN'T WORTH THAT AGGRAVATION YOU'LL FIND OUT I SWEAR YOU WILL!

They pay no attention.

OH SHE ARST ME TER FUCKIN' REACH I'LL TELL YOU WOT I CAUGHT! THERE WASN'T A MOMENT NOT A MOMENT I WOULDN'T DO AGAIN ON'Y THIS TIME I'D DO IT WIVOUT THE SHOUTIN' AND THE 'GIMME THIS' AND THE 'DO THAT' I WOULDN'T WORRY ABAHT THAT AN' IF IT MEANT SERVIN' THEN I'D FUCKIN' SERVE YOU – YOU GOT TO KNUCKLE UNDER. I TELL YOU YORE TOO YOUNG ONCE YOU 'ELD YORE BABIES IN YORE ARMS THERE ISN'T 'BOY' THIS OR 'GIRL' THAT THERE'S –

Still they circle.

I TELL YOU I DON'T GIVE A FUCK WOT ANY OF YOU SAY IT OUGHT TER BE BEAUTIFUL RIGHT? SO GIVE IT A CHANCE! GIVE THAT BOY A FUCKIN' CHANCE CHRIST THEY WAS MAD FER EACH UVVER. YOU JOHN *YOU* DINCH YOU SEE 'EM GIVE EACH UVVER THE EYE? NOW WASN'T THAT NICE EH? I TELL YOU BACK OFF

WOSS SO WRONG WIV THAT?
WOSS WRONG?

But all the kids are in a sense enjoying it.

(*To* SHARON:) AN' YORE AS BAD
YOO ARE! WHERE'S THE FUCKIN'
'ARM IN A BOY WIV A GEL EH?
YOU TELL ME! YOU GIVE ME
SOME ANSWERS 'COS I'M TELLIN'
YOO I DON'T REGRET IT WHERE'S
THE 'ARM? WHERE?

SHARON: There.

SUZE: PLE-EASE!!!!

JOHN: Want some a' this then Steve?

STEVE: Much as yoo got prat.

SUZE: PLEASE FER GAWD'S SAKE
GIVE IT A REST! PLEASE!

SHARON: Yore wastin' yore time Suze. Iss
wot they bin' waitin' for. I tell yer. They
fuckin' enjoy it.

CAROL: GO ON STEPHEN 'AMMER
'IM! 'AMMER 'IM! 'AMMER 'IM!

SUZE: CAROL DON'T!

*And they clinch. A violent struggle in
which they fall. JOHN, in the clinch,
grinds the bottle into STEPHEN's
genitals. STEVE screams wildly.
SHARON is comforting SUZE. CAROL
aghast. JOHN backs off from him, the
now bloody bottle in his hand.*

JOHN: NOW JUS' LEAVE OFF OF ME
O.K? NOW JUS' YOU STOP YORE
FUCKIN' RACKET O.K? LEAVE
OFF!

SUZE: Oh my Christ.

SHARON: Doctor. Chrace gedda doctor.
Phone. Gedda –

JOHN: Keep away from that fuckin' phone
you 'ear?

TRACY *moves.*

KEEP AWAY OR YOU GET SOME A'
THIS! I TELL YOU I'VE 'AD ALL I
NEED! MESSIN' ME UP AN'
CONFUSIN' ME! YOU WAN'ED A
MAN DINCHER? WELL YOU GOT
ONE AINCHER? ME EH? WELL OO
LAID 'IM AHT THEN?

A rustle of movement from the women.

KEEP AWAY FROM THAT PHONE!

I'LL LAY WASTE TO ANYONE OO
FUCKIN' MOVES O.K? I AM IN
CHARGE!

LEROY: John –

JOHN: I am in charge you 'ear. I don't want
nobody moved I don' want no Law called
I don' wan' nuffing I am in charge an' I
want fings ter stay just as they are O.K?
O.K?

CAROL: *Sharon . . .*

SHARON: Oh donch yoo come ter me gel.
Time fer comin ter me was some time
back donch yer fink. I tell yer. If we don't
do it to them they'll do it ter themselves.
Like bleed'n dogs they'll bite theirselves
ter death like dogs or fuckin' scorpions.
Yore wastin' yore time Carol an' if you
won' lissen then yoo'll still waste it.

JOHN: KEEP AWAY FROM ME YOU
SLAG DONCH YOO START ON ME
I'M IN CHARGE I TOLD YER
NOBODY GETS NEAR ME
NOBODY BOVVERS ME I AM IN
CHARGE THIS IS 'OW THINGS ARE
GONNER STAY! (*Shaking.*) I saw this
slag at a bus stop. Follered 'er 'ome an'
all. Kept away from women. I'll give 'em
kept away. I was all right there son I can
tell yer. No problem. No problem.

Looking round at all of them.

WELL COME ON OO'S GONNER
START IT EH? OO'S GONNER BE
THE FIRST! COME ON THEN YOU
USELESS GETS COME ON!

SHARON: Nobody's gonner fuckin' start
it. You started it. You finished it. An'
when you 'ave finished it. When you've
smashed every single fuckin' fing you can
lay yore 'and on, when you've bought an'
made war on an' fucked an' borrered an'
used up the ol' bleed'n planet then we'll
come in. An' we'll start all over again.
From Adam an' fuckin' Eve. Becos we
'ave *finished* with the likes a' you. We 'ave
finished.

JOHN: WELL FINISH ME THEN
CANCHER? FUCKIN' FINISH ME
PLEASE!!!

*And he falls to his knees, the anger finally
turned in on himself, stabbing at the carpet
with the broken bottle, used up, broken
himself.*

SUZE: You. Tracy. Gedda doctor. 999.

TRACY *moves to the phone.* CAROL *goes to* STEVE.

CAROL: Bandage 'im.

SHARON: Carol –

CAROL: Shut up! Stephen . . .

STEVE: Carol . . .

CAROL: Sssssh.

STEVE: Woss . . .

CAROL: Lay quiet lovey.

She takes him in her arms.

SUZE: You should a kept yore fuckin' chrap shut.

CAROL: Giss a sheet Suze.

SUZE: Why joo –

CAROL: *Please!* Tear up a sheet or sunnink.

SUZE: Yeah. I'll . . . I don' fuckin' *understand* you kids . . . I fought.

CAROL: Fuck understandin' willyer? Giss a sheet.

SUZE *goes to a back cupboard.*

STEVE: Am I O.K?

CAROL: You'll be all right.

STEVE: You all right?

CAROL: I'm O.K.

Pause.

Us two are O.K. I promise yer.

SUZE *comes back with the sheet.* TRACY *looks up from the phone.*

TRACY: They don' fuckin' answer.

CAROL: Honest Stevie love. We'll be all right.

Winding the sheet on him.

TRACY: Well carm on then less 'ave yer!

STEVE: I shoun't foller girls should I though?

CAROL: Don' listen ter no-one Stevie not eiver side a' the fuckin' fence. You foller oo yoo like.

TRACY: WELL CARM ON FER FUCK'S SAKE! DON' ANYBODY FUCKIN' CARE?

STEVE: Will I be all right?

CAROL: You'll be fine Stevie. Honest.

Holding him close.

Thass my boy. An' then we'll meet won't we? Eh? Somewhere where there ain't no ovver people eh? Somewhere away from the lot of it. We'll meet up. 'Course we will. An' we'll go out. We'll go out ter places. Films an' 'at. Pubs. Fer a jrink. An' we'll meet all the fuckin' time. We'll talk an' all. We'll talk non-stop. Honest. An' I'll look amazin' for yer Stevie. Honest. They won't fuckin' know me nor you neiver we'll be a regular couple, we'll be a beautiful couple honest. Beautiful. No-one in ver wide fuckin' world'll know us.

SHARON: They ain' answerin' Carol.

CAROL: They will Sharon.

Angry and tear-stained she looks across at her friend.

They will.

Back by the phone. TRACY *drops it allowing the receiver to swing.* SUZE *stands among her pictures.* SHARON *smokes and* CAROL *bends over* STEVE. *The lights slowly fade so that the last thing we see on the stage are two naked figures. It is –*

The End

TRIAL RUN

List of Characters

BILLY
GANGE
JOHN
TWIGS
JANE
SAM
SMILER
A POLICE OFFICER *heard but not seen*

Trial Run was first presented on tour by the Oxford Playhouse Company and then at the Young Vic Theatre, London on 25th February 1980, with the following cast:

BILLY	Renu Setna
GANGE	Art Malik
JOHN	Nicholas Lyndhurst
TWIGS	Saiward Green
JANE	Kim Clifford
SAM	Nigel Planer
SMILER	Dominic Letts

Directed by Nicholas Kent
Designed by Stephanie Howard
Lighting by Raymond Cross

The play is set in the basement packing room of a Woolworth's store in Hounslow. The time is the present.

Act One

The basement of a medium-sized store – in fact F.W. Woolworth of Hounslow. There is only one way out – through a door back right, which leads to a small hall, away from which a narrow staircase slopes up quite steeply. This bit of the basement is usually used as a packing room. It is littered, not to say piled high, with shabby cardboard boxes, and the only furniture in use by those who at present occupy the place is several large tea-chests. Some of the boxes have been opened and the consumer durables they contained are visible, but on the whole the set should be a desolate sea of cardboard.
GANGE, *a young British-born Sikh, is standing centre stage holding a revolver.* BILLY, *a man of thirty-eight, English mother, Indian father, is at the door. He too holds a revolver. Otherwise, as the lights go up, we see two shop-girls of about sixteen –* TWIGS, *a fat girl and* JANE, *a prettier girl, a security guard of nineteen called* JOHN *and a student of twenty-five called* SAM.

GANGE: 'S real!

TWIGS: We can see that.

GANGE: See?

He fires the revolver into the air.

Carm on Billy. Show 'em yores!

BILLY: Oh fuck off can't you please old chap.

He speaks to the youth in Punjabi. When he speaks in an Indian dialect his voice has none of the complicated self mockery he considers necessary when speaking English.

We are in need of a victim. Sorry – accused.

GANGE: 'E's a trier in' e? Donch yoo never give up?

He moves.

Woch yoo fink it'll be next eh lads? Loud 'ailers? Poison gas? While me an' Sunshine 'ere is amusin' ourselves vey're prob'ly phonin' Noo York ter get a secret plan a' the buildin'. They've probably asked the Ayatollah Khomeini ter intervene.

BILLY: Just so long as they don't involve Lord Goodman we shall be all right. If they involve Lord Goodman we are

finished. They will swing him down on a rope and batter down the door with him. They will fill him full of exploding gas and float him down the stair well. They –

GANGE: Well get on wiv it.

BILLY: But you see nobody wants to be a victim. Isn't that absurd? In an apparently Christian country we can't find a volunteer victim? We have a jury, we have witnesses, we have a courtroom. After a great deal of effort we have really quite a promising little trial but we don't have a victim. I must ask you once again as I am empowered to do, doesn't anyone want to be a victim? Sorry – accused.

TWIGS: Canch yoo let 'er go? She's 'ighly strung.

GANGE: Is she bleedin'? Thass the question? Is she bleedin'?

TWIGS: She's not well.

JANE: I ain't well.

GANGE: But she ain't bleedin'? Is she? Now – me an' Billy 'ere. We're bleedin'. 'En't we fuckface?

BILLY parodies the English idea of the Asian. Curry and chips stuff. He does it frighteningly well.

BILLY: It is so. In our hearts we are bleeding. Oh sahib we are bleeding.

GANGE: 'As she bin 'it on the 'ead?

JANE: Give over you.

GANGE: If you're white – you're all right.
If you're brown – stick around.
But if you're black – oh brother –
Get back get back get back.

TWIGS: 'Er 'ead's bad. She 'as bad 'eadaches.

BILLY: Don't admit to signs of weakness. Otherwise you will find yourself in the dock old girl. We're about to make illness a punishable crime down here.

SAM: Look I'll be your damn victim!

GANGE: Oh no. Oh no! (*Going to him.*) 'E tolj yer. You ain't gonner be no victim. You gonner be the judge.

BILLY: Here come de judge!

GANGE: We can't seem ter get this inter yore 'ead can we? It is really provin' unbearably difficult.

SAM: I told you – I don't approve of judges. I don't want to be one.

GANGE: 'Ark at 'im! 'Don't approve.' I mean you talk like a fuckin' judge you do mate. Always givin' us yore opinions incher? Well you talked yorself into a job mush.

SAM: Listen – I won't be –

GANGE pushes him towards a tea chest. There is a lot of needle between these two, of a purely instinctive kind.

GANGE: You will son. You'll be a good boy. 'Ere's yore seat. (*Pushing him down on it.*) An' 'ere's yore 'at! (*Cramming another box on his head.*) An' 'ere, Einstein, is yore gravel. (*Giving him a roll of cardboard.*)

SAM: Gavel.

GANGE: I don't give a fuck woch yoo wanner call it son. Bash on that box.

SAM: Look -

GANGE: BASH IT!

SAM bashes it.

RIGHT! (*Turning to the others.*) Nah. When Sam 'ere bashes 'is gravel: we will 'ave silence in court. (SAM *bashes it.*) 'Owever – 'e will on'y blow it at certain prescribed intervals. This is a court of law didn't you know? Things are done damn well properly here. And the judge is only allowed to bash his gravel when my young friend and I so instruct him. This is known as Judge's Rules.

GANGE fires his revolver.

And what he just did is known as precedent you see. That is what we call tradition you see. That is the reminder of your liberties. Yes?

GANGE fires again.

GANGE: The door!

BILLY runs for it. He shouts up.

BILLY: Any nearer and I fire. O.K.? (*Holding up his revolver.*) And don't try to talk to us. Not yet. O.K.? We are coming up with a list of demands.

TWIGS: They wanner fly to Bahrein.

JANE: Take Woolies wiv 'em an' all.

BILLY: That's it. That's it constable. Back. Back. Back. Now that way you're nice.

Very nice. Very nice. And we can hear every move you make.

He shuts the door. He fires his revolver. Instead of bullets – water. It appears to be a water pistol. He smiles.

Your policemen are wonderful.

JOHN: Well they're there mate. Ain't they?

GANGE: Vey will go away when vey seen our demands.

BILLY: They will burst out singing. They will be so damn happy when they have seen our demands. Because you see – our demands will be very carefully framed. They won't be the usual rubbish about the release of the Islington 500. They will be entirely and utterly reasonable.

SAM: Listen –

GANGE: Get the judge a chair fatso. Ainch yoo got no fuckin' manners?

TWIGS: Charmin'!

TWIGS isn't impressed by GANGE. As a result of this he quite likes her.

GANGE: Let the court rise!

No-one rises. Perhaps he's too amiable about it.

RISE YOU RUDE SODS!

They rise.

And nah. Ver judge will sit dahn. Won' 'e?

In the end SAM sits.

JOHN: I reckon the two of you's barmy.

BILLY: Ye-eas?

JOHN: I reckon you ain't got a notion as to why yore 'ere or woch yore doin' or why you bin so bloody –

BILLY: Doesn't he audition well?

JOHN: Uh?

BILLY: I think it was the tone of your voice. A little whining. A little self-justifying. I thought you sounded like a –

JOHN: Like a wot?

BILLY: Like a man in the dock or something old boy.

JOHN: Look –

BILLY: That's the tone of voice I mean old boy. Like that old chap. Just like that.

The part's yours.

TWIGS: Woss 'e on abaht?

JANE: Search me.

JOHN: Look you two. I ain't done anyfing ter you an' –

BILLY: Marvellous. Marvellous. We don't need to hear any more. Marvellous. Super. It. You're it. I think as far as we're concerned you're . . . it.

GANGE: I got a better idea. Why don't we –

BILLY: O.K.?

JOHN *turns to* GANGE.

JOHN: Wot is this nah?

BILLY: You're guilty. Sorry. Charged. Sorry – you're perfect. I mean you work. You really will be super. In this court anyway.

GANGE: On account vis is a magistrate's court eh? Magistrates. Thass us. An' if yore black . . . get back . . . an' if yore . . .

JOHN: OO SAID I WAS BLACK?

GANGE: This is a good point son.

But BILLY *turns it away from* GANGE's *slightly more human response.*

BILLY: My God we've got a problem here young man. Oh my Golly Gosh. Oh my Dal and Ladies' Fingers. Oh my Brinjal Bhaji what a problem. He's guilty but he isn't black. Well. Don't tell me. I know. I'm working on it. I'm working on it. No no. He's charged but he isn't black. He's accused but he isn't black. In the which case there is just a chance that he may be innocent. That is to say white. But that is what British justice is all about.

SAM: Look I've never heard such a load of – (*Stops.*) Look what is with this? What are you –

GANGE: Oh fuck off you. You're the judge. 'Ave some fuckin' manners.

JOHN: Look. I ain't 'ostile ter colour. Am not. I ain't –

BILLY: You ain't black that's for sure old boy. And that is why we're going to give you a chance. We're not just going to charge you oh no no no no. We're going to let you hear all the evidence against you and we're going to give you a chance

to say what you think of it and we're going to call expert testimony and we're going to have a public inquiry and by Golly Gosh old man by the time you've finished you are going to have had the fairest fucking trial in the history of the world. Frankly you'll be a lot better off then if you'd never *been* charged in the first place. My God it's going to be like Miami Florida. I keep telling you old boy we're going to do it *properly* down here.

TWIGS: They're talkin' to yer.

GANGE: Oh fer Chris' –

JANE: *Twigs* –

Everyone freezes. We hear a voice coming from a landing at the top of the stairs. Not amplified in any way, a normal human voice. But, somehow, it sounds a long way away.

VOICE: If you want food or drink we can let you have that.

Pause.

We can let you have that.

A pause. Then GANGE *rushes to the door. He opens it but only half-way.*

GANGE: Lissen. We on'y been in 'ere five hours. Woch yoo 'fink vis is – an 'otel? Blimey. We don' wan' elevenses mush. An' we don' wan' no coppers passin' dahn no explodin' jam rols neiver. O.K.? So fuck off an' leave us in peace cancher? We are formulatin' our demands. An' if anyone interferes vere will be ve odd dead body dahn 'ere. O.K.?

BILLY *joins him at the door. He seems more relaxed about the occasion.*

BILLY: Oh – and we want to see a priest. A Moslem priest.

GANGE: An' a Cafolic priest an' all.

BILLY: And a dentist. We need a dentist urgently own here.

GANGE: And a fireman.

BILLY: And an account executive. We absolutely must see an account executive. Because our image is wrong. We are finding it difficult to explain the complexity of our position. And an accountant also we need. Because we are worried about our tax position you see.

GANGE: Woss 'e sayin'?

BILLY: He says he'll get us a priest. He wants to know if we have a particular priest in mind.

GANGE: A small one. One that dispenses Coca-fuckin'-Cola.

BILLY: We want a Marxist priest. There are a few in South America. We want a priest who can call God to account. O.K.? One who can persuade the old sod to be a bit on the reliable side. And don't forget the accountant.

GANGE: AN' LEAVE US ALONE YOU ARSE'OLES. O.K.?

They shut the door.

TWIGS: Wot do you want eh?

BILLY: So many things my dear we want. Things in here. Things out there. Important things. Unimportant things. Things for the world and things for ourselves. Things to stop the suffering out there and things to stop the suffering in here. Nostrums. Placebos. Things to stop our mouths and our eyes and our hearts. Things to . . . silt up the responses.

GANGE: Oi fuck face. Yore ve accused. Stand there.

BILLY: He must. He's on trial so he must.

SAM: Look suppose I said he was not guilty. As a matter of fact suppose I said –

TWIGS: I wouldn't mate. They might get a bit dodgy.

BILLY: What a sensible girl.

GANGE: She is aware vat we are crazed men of violence oo will stop at nuffink ter get the fings they desire. I.e. we are almost as bad as the average copper.

BILLY *points at* GANGE.

BILLY: Counsel for the prosecution.

TWIGS: Wot are yoo then?

JANE: The usher.

BILLY: I too am counsel for the prosecution. We have two you see. Because I'm a bit more tricky than he is. I'm generally agreed to be a nastier kettle of beans you see.

SAM: You must have a counsel for the defence.

GANGE: FUCK OFF YOU! OO TOLJ YOO TER OPEN YORE MOUF?

YORE THE JUDGE THASS WOCH YOO ARE! SIT THERE AN' FUCKIN' JUDGE O.K?

JANE: Wot did yoo do? Why was they chasin' yoo in 'ere eh?

BILLY: We didn't say please and thankyou. (*To all of them.*) How about 'We the undersigned – being the West London Action Group for Complete Equality Between Everybody, demand an immediate and complete withdrawal of Mrs. Thatcher, M.P. for Barnet.'

SAM: From where?

BILLY: Well from Barnet. Initially. And eventually from circulation. 'We also request that Chief Constable Alderton and his friend and fellow conspirator David Macnee of the Metropolitan Police be required to stand headfirst in a bucket of something or other while a hand-picked group from the Anti-Nazi League read and sing selections from the work of Herbert Marcuse.'

JOHN: They're political. I told you they was political.

BILLY: Oh we are. We are highly political. We are trying to abduct the Israeli Ambassador. Which is why we ended up in Woolworth's in Hounslow. We thought the Israeli Ambassador would be in here buying himself a pair of Winfield pyjamas. Check the door.

GANGE *crosses, half opens it.*

GANGE: Two coppers at the top a' the stairs. Fuck all else.

BILLY: They're probably tunnelling. (*To* JOHN.) Your name please.

JOHN: Listen –

BILLY: And you will please to stand there.

GANGE: It bein' ver dock.

BILLY: Your name.

JOHN: This is schoopid. I –

BILLY: YOUR NAME!

Pause.

SAM: Objection.

GANGE: FUCK OFF!

TWIGS: I thought you was leavin' it aht?

BILLY: Not at all. He has a role to play. He

understands all that. A good judge. Awfully good. Top hole. What is your objection my lord?

SAM: Counsel is bullying the witness.

BILLY: He isn't a witness – he's the accused. If your Lordship pleases.

SAM: Says who?

BILLY: Says me.

GANGE: Objection a load a' rubbish. Proceed.

JOHN: Latham.

BILLY: First names.

JOHN: John Paul.

BILLY: Age?

JOHN: Nineteen.

BILLY: Occupation?

JOHN: Security Guard.

BILLY: Weight?

JOHN: Ten stone.

BILLY: Qualifications?

GANGE: Shaky.

JOHN: You wot?

BILLY: Mr Latham – what made you decide to become a Security Guard?

JOHN: Er – (*Pause.*) I dunno.

BILLY: Exhibit A my Lord. Exhibit A in the case for the prosecution. Here is a man who is walking around Woolworth's in a black peaked hat and a uniform with silver buttons on it – a man who looks as if he's dressed up for the annual general meeting of the British Nazi Movement and he says he doesn't know why he's wearing the uniform. It is our contention that ignorance is always a crime but in this case –

SAM: Why don' we hear the rest of the evidence?

TWIGS: Bold incher?

GANGE: Watch it!

BILLY: Don't you realise my Lord that the central part of the evidence against this man is liable to be himself and that the more we find out about him the more damn likely we are to hang him. I therefore move that we find out as little as

possible about him on the grounds that any more information can only incriminate him further.

SAM: Objection overruled.

Pause.

BILLY: Ah. Are you afraid that we will shoot him now? Are you afraid that we are a couple of psychopaths? Are you afraid that we are like those terrorists you read about? Eh? You know – the ones who should be shot and tortured and made to listen to their dying children's screams, the monsters who are beyond the pale, the people who do such beastly frightful things that my God they should have a few kilograms of creosote jammed up their rear quarters. Is that what you take us for?

TWIGS: You prob'ly got a grievance. Right?

BILLY: GOT IT IN ONE SISTER! And we are human beings too. Aren't we?

GANGE: No. We're sub'uman we are.

BILLY: I'm going to accept your objection.

SAM: After all I am the judge.

BILLY: You are getting more like the judge. If I allow you to get away with any more you'll probably go out and buy a wig and send me down for two years. Do you know Brian Canham?

SAM: Never heard of him.

BILLY: Oh you should meet him. He's a magistrate in Ealing.

GANGE: A lovely boy. (*At the door.*) I TOLJ YER TER FUCK OFF!

BILLY: Anything?

GANGE: Same two geezers.

BILLY: Oh tell them we mean – (GANGE *fires.*) – business.

GANGE: They went. Surprise surprise.

Reloading the gun.

JOHN: Look if you wanner know – vis iss a good job.

BILLY: What is?

JOHN: Security. Iss a good job in fact.

BILLY: And what does it offer?

JOHN: It offers . . .

GANGE: Security.

JOHN: Iss useful.

TWIGS: 'E's no bleedin' use at all is John.

JOHN: 'Ang abaht.

JANE: Well. Look at 'im.

BILLY: Witnesses will please not to interrupt the proceedings of the court.

TWIGS: Should a' bought an alsation instead they should.

The girls giggle. BILLY *paces, warming to his role. Much legal flourishing.*

Now Mr. Latham – are you married?

JOHN: No.

JANE: No chance.

BILLY: That is a point in your favour. The possibility that you might reproduce yourself I and my learned friend would find extremely disturbing.

GANGE: Oh less 'ammer someone, I'm fuckin' –

BILLY: Sssh.

The violence in GANGE *is more natural. It subsides as soon as raised.*

There. Occasionally my learned friend becomes carried away. You must understand that he's only just down from the trees and so his passions tend to the primitive. How long have you been in your present employment Mr. Latham?

JOHN: Two years.

BILLY: And previous to that you were –

JOHN: Out a' work.

BILLY: And prior to being unemployed you were –

JOHN: At school.

BILLY: Where you obtained the usual G.C.E.s and so forth . . .

JOHN: No.

BILLY: Your parents Mr. Latham – are they living?

JOHN: Yeh.

BILLY: Your father's profession?

JOHN: Clerk.

BILLY: Mother's profession?

JOHN: Uh?

BILLY: Brothers and sisters?

JOHN: None.

BILLY: Car?

JOHN: No.

BILLY: Flat?

JOHN: Look –

BILLY: Holidays?

JOHN: Woss the –

BILLY: Sex?

JOHN: Leave off.

BILLY: Happy?

JOHN: Woch yoo fink?

BILLY: Oh I'm sure you're delirious Mr. Latham. I'm sure you're delirious. (*Moving to the girls.*) Actually lady and lady of the jury it is possible that the more one gets to know Mr. Latham the fonder one might become of him. It would be folly to be wise in such a uniform. You may cross-examine the accused witness while I vet the jury.

SAM: Objection.

BILLY: Ye-es?

SAM: Counsel is armed.

BILLY: Yes.

SAM: This may intimidate the witness.

BILLY: Ye-es.

SAM: Counsel is prejudiced.

BILLY: Ye-es.

SAM: Counsel is fucking dangerous.

BILLY: And I?

SAM: Look . . . you're . . .

BILLY: I'm a nice sort of Indian chap eh? Oh I'm a kind of good sport old boy. I'm a well turned out sort of feller me lad. What on earth is a nice fellow like me doing in a place like this? It's fairly impossible that I feel anything the way he does or that I'm in any danger of catching the . . . psychopathic rage with which he seems afflicted after all I'm in carpet slippers oh my Goodness Gracious me anything you say sahib what's in order old bean? Polo? Polo or something? Do you think? Eh? (*Suddenly savage.*) Get on with it.

GANGE: I'll tell them sods aht there shall I?

BILLY: I told you out there or in here what's the bloody difference?

GANGE: WELL SHALL I TELL 'EM NAH EH? WE BIN 'ERE FIVE FUCKIN' HOURS I MIGHT AS WELL LET 'EM INTER THE SECRET!

BILLY: I TOLD YOU IT WON'T MAKE ANY DIFFERENCE!

Pause.

We're having fun down here.

GANGE: Look –

BILLY: Interrogate him.

GANGE *turns the anger he was going to use on talking to the policemen outside on to* JOHN. BILLY *is very good at controlling this boy . . .*

GANGE: RIGHT YOU CUNT WHERE WAS YOU ON OCTOBER THE FIRTEENF LAST EH?

SAM: Look –

GANGE: Where was you?

JOHN: I –

GANGE: WHERE WAS YOU?

JOHN: Listen –

GANGE: I DEF'NITELY SAW YOU CUNT! I DEF'NITELY SAW YOU ON OCTOBER THE FIRTEENF! YOU WAS DEF'NITELY THERE!

JOHN: Where?

BILLY: You don't know? You don't know where you are supposed to have been? My God. This is more serious than I had supposed.

JOHN: I dunno woch yore on abaht.

BILLY: And *that* is what *we* are on about. Mr. Latham.

GANGE: DID YOU OR DID YOU NOT GIVE EVIDENCE AGAINST ME AT BARNET MAGISTRATE'S COURT ON OCTOBER THE THIRTEENTH LAST? ANSWER YES OR YES!

JOHN: I –

Pause.

SAM: Yes. Yes of course he did.

BILLY: He's *humouring* us. We don't like that one little bit. He's *humouring* us.

SAM: If you say he did he did.

BILLY: Objection. Judge is abandoning wig.

SAM: Objection. I object to being the judge. I don't want the job.

BILLY: Judges can't resign. Not here.

TWIGS: I dunno woch yore on at John for.

GANGE: WELL CARM ON YOU CUNT ANSWER THE QUESTION? DIDJER OR DIDN'T YER?

JOHN: YES IF YOU SAY SO YES! YES GIVE EVIDENCE AGAINST YOU IF YOU SAY SO! (*Looking straight at* GANGE.) Yes yes yes yes.

BILLY: Excellent.

But GANGE *turns on* BILLY.

GANGE: I DON' SEE WOSS SO FUCKIN' EXCELLENT! WHY DON'T WE TELL THE SODS AHT THERE WOT WE WANT?

BILLY: Well. What do we want? How much do we want? Do we even want the same damn things? Eh?

GANGE: You know wot I want.

BILLY: Oh I'm not against your asking for anything. If you really think it's that simple you ask. I've no objection at all. But it's not a toyshop out there you know. Take time. Take time over your demands. Ask for something you really want – that is to say – something they won't give you.

GANGE: I dunno woch yoo want you mad bastard.

BILLY: I am considering. And at the moment it upsets me to think of involving anyone outside in the decision. Down here we have a very promising little action. I'm enjoying it.

Like a solicitor to a worried client, blinding him with science perhaps.

The case is going well. Rule number one of all police forces is always obtain a confession. From the accused. If necessary by force. Even if he can prove he was in Katmandu on the day the offence was committed at least you have a confession that he committed the crime and even if he is malicious enough to want to change his confession at a later date you have at least got the beginnings of a case. The accused is guilty. It is now time to hear the evidence against him.

But GANGE *has crossed to the door. He shouts up at them.*

GANGE: LISSEN YOU LOT. I WANT SOMEONE! I WANT SOMEONE IN PARTICULAR! 'IS NAME'S EVANS O.K? 'IS NUMBER'S 45632 AND 'E GIVE EVIDENCE AGAINST ME AT BARNET LAST YEAR ALL RIGHT? NAH NEVER MIND MY NAME BUT 'E WAS THERE! YOU'LL KNOW THE GEEZER! 'E'S FROM LEYTONSTONE! I WAN' 'IM DAHN 'ERE AN' THEN THIS LOT CAN CLEAR OFF O.K? (*No answer.*) GEDDIT? (*He slams the door.*)

BILLY: Well I'm sure we can add a few more to that later on. We can ask for the entire editorial staff of the Sun newspaper and we can ask for fifteen sausage rolls and the head of Peter Sellers and a copy of the Koran bound in gold my God we have the whole night ahead of us. Don't think it's finished.

GANGE: Well. Now you know.

TWIGS: They won't give you no copper. They stick tergevver do coppers.

BILLY: Well then – we'll just have to make do with the one we've got – won't we?

A nasty moment. Attention focusses on JOHN.

I call the counsel for the prosecution.

GANGE: Sah!

BILLY: What is your name please?

GANGE: Fuck off.

BILLY: You are Russian?

GANGE: Up yores.

BILLY: You are not Russian.

GANGE: Get *on* wiv it.

To BILLY *in Punjabi. They speak.* GANGE *seems to be pleading with him about something but* BILLY *'s relaxed, playing him.*

Why can't we jus' –

BILLY: Sssh. Sssh. You have to make it last. (*Close to him.*) Don't think I'm not serious. I'm perfectly serious. I'm known to be a very serious person. There are just some other things I want to work on. I'm behind you. I keep telling you. I'm behind you. (*Swivelling round to* SAM.) The learned judge has got his eye on the door and I would beg the learned judge not to continue with this gesture if the learned judge wishes to preserve his . . . er . . . goolies intact because the learned prosecuting counsel is carrying a weapon which, in the event of any movement in the direction of or tending towards the door would most probably be led or made to appear to be pointing the direction of the aforementioned goolies, thus and therefore ex parte necessitas tending to the loss or damage or at least certain impairment of the said goolies by the said armed weapon and rendering the owner of the aforementioned goolies gooli-less or without goolies.

SAM *stops.*

O.K? (*He turns to* GANGE.) Now. State your age.

GANGE: Five hundred and ninety.

BILLY: Very good. Your occupation?

GANGE: Circus midget.

BILLY: Address?

GANGE: Runway two 'Eafrow Airport.

BILLY: Hobbies?

GANGE: Woodwork.

BILLY: Ambition?

GANGE: Ter be an air 'ostess.

BILLY: And would you like to request a record?

GANGE: Not at this time my lord.

BILLY: On what grounds?

GANGE: On the grounds that it might incriminate me.

BILLY: You are ashamed of your taste in music?

GANGE: I am not proud of it.

BILLY: Tell me lance corporal – have you ever now or in the past listened to or bought the records of or become involved in any way in an auditory sense with the group 'Abba'?

GANGE: IT WAS ON'Y ONCE! I WAS LED ON YORE WORSHIP! (*Only doing it because* BILLY *likes it.*) O.K?

BILLY: Does the learned judge wish to cross-examine?

SAM: He doesn't look like a midget.

BILLY: Lady and lady of the jury the counsel for the prosectuion is an experienced black person. He has been a black person since the day he was born – in fact lady and lady of the jury there has not been a single time in his brief life when he has been anything other than a little bit less than white. Now I want you to bear in mind that in this matter of his being or not being a 'circus midget' we have only the word of the learned judge against the word of my learned friend. Now I think you have to ask yourself a very serious question here. *If* – as I have pointed out to you – it is a question of aut unus aut unus – one or the other – you are going to have to make up your mind whether to believe someone who is, if I may say so, a pillar, a rock, a sine qua non of our judicial system or to trust in the word of one who, good chap though he may be, is quite clearly not of our race or system or culture. Not convinced?

Very close to the two girls. Very much the American lawyer now – Perry Mason stuff.

Well if I can't appeal to your intellect let me appeal to your baser natures. (*Indicating* GANGE.) I want to *beg* you. I want to *implore* you not to send this young man to prison. And I want you to consider very carefully before you proceed to judge him perjured that we would be sending him into a closed community that is already in danger of having what I might describe as its ethnic character swamped and muddied by the inroads of cultures and traditions alien to it. I am speaking, lady and lady of the jury, of something as fundamental and basic and important as the ethnic character of our penal institutions. You see I want to see the prisons of this country preserve what I am proud of actually, I want to see them a place where white men and white women can exercise and sew mailbags and play table-tennis and watch the Open University on

television without having the basic nature of their community subverted by a load of nig-nogs. I want to keep Pentonville white. So I want you to bear that in mind and I want you to look at my learned friend and ask yourself very seriously the question 'Is he or is he not a circus midget' bearing in mind that if he *is* a circus midget we stand a chance just a remote sliver of an opportunity of saving one of the last remaining bastions of our cultural heritage free from the poison of racial miscegenation. Go on. Go on. Look at him. Isn't he shrinking visibly? Isn't he getting smaller though?

TWIGS: Yore a fruitcake you are.

SAM: My God I only wish he was.

BILLY: My Lord – irony is wasted on the lower orders.

GANGE: I wish ter change my statement.

BILLY: Ye-es.

GANGE: When I said I was a midget I was readin' my notes upside dahn. I should a' said I was an interior designer. They're takin' their fuckin' time en't they?

BILLY: Listen. Don't worry about what they're doing all the time. Worry about what *we're* doing.

GANGE: I s'pose 'e might be out. On jooty. Eh?

SAM: Your Constable Evans.

GANGE: My Constable Evans.

SAM: What did he send you down for? Sus or what?

BILLY: Golly!

SAM: Was it that?

GANGE: Fuck off you.

SAM: What did he send you down for?

GANGE: SIX MONTHS THASS WOT 'E SENT ME DAHN FOR!

SAM: I'm sorry.

BILLY: Oh don't apologise. It's not your fault old bean. (*Indicates* JOHN.) It's his fault.

GANGE: Oh you fuck off an' all cancher?

BILLY: You really think they'll send him.

TWIGS: You two bruvvers or wot?

GANGE: Blood bruvvers we are en't we?

SAM: Was this to do with the Southall –

GANGE: Oh yore such a fuckin' expert you are aincher? Yore a real fly on the wall you are. Wot makes you such a fuckin' expert on me eh? 'Ow come yore so bleed'n knowledgeable? As a matter of a fact it was nowhere near West London. As a matter of fact I was appre'ended in Stow-on-the-fuckin'-Wold. O.K? Satisfied? That fit does it?

SAM: Look I only –

BILLY: Tell them my son. Tell them what you have suffered already my life.

SAM: O.K. O.K.

BILLY: I'm afraid I don't need that actually old boy. I'm afraid I don't need people like you telling me I'm living in bloody Nazi Germany or something. Because I'm not, so please bloody forget that O.K? What do you want? God. He's got a point about you.

GANGE: There I am in Stow-on-ver-Wold. In my 'at. Nice as you please. The birds are singin' an' the flowers are peepin' up out their 'oles and the thatched cottages are bein' repaired at great cost to the in'abitants. The road is deserted. It stretches away inter the 'orizon abso-fuckin'-lutely packed wiv' 'ed'ogs an' bunny rabbits an' fieldmice an' moles an' voles an' badgers an' toads in lit'l blue jackets an' schriped chrousers. It is – I do not kid – an idyllic scene. Then be'ind me I 'ear 'em. Ten fuckin' police vans innit? Green jobs wiv bars on the winder. They screen up be'ind me, narrerly missin' a vole an' out jumps vese coppers. Wearin' crash 'elmets, goggles, masks, flippers, ear muffs, scabbards – the bloody lot. They grope their way over ver road and hail me.

BILLY: Right.

GANGE: 'Excuse me young Asian person in chraditional 'eadgear!' sez the biggest a' these p'licemen, oo is wearin' a kind a' steel box toped wiv barbed wire, 'Excuse me!' 'e sez, 'but we are lookin' for the demonstration.' 'Wot demonstration?' I sez, 'this is Stow-on-the-fuckin'-Wold this is mate. There ain't no demonstration 'ere!' An' I point dahn the dusty white road alive with tiny mammals. 'Well,' sez this p'liceman from deep wivin 'is protective clovin' 'I was told there was a demonstration 'ereabouts.' 'Search me!' I sez. So 'e did. 'E looks in my ears an' under my arms an' up my nose an' then 'e finds it.

BILLY: 'It' being –

GANGE: The offensive weapon. Concealed in my underwear. Curled up, shyly, under a bush. But quite obviously capable of inflictin' severe damage on a white woman. So 'e –

SAM: Look whatever you were done for and wherever it happened – I was only trying to understand. Is that so wrong?

BILLY: Trying to get to the root of the problem. Quite obviously my learned friend is not a person at all but a problem. Coming as he does from miles across the seas he finds it difficult to make the complex series of adjustments necessary for full integration into white society. He finds it difficult to come to terms with the superstructure of the host community. And, in turn, this is aggravated by the fact that the host community's police keep bashing him over the bonce with truncheons, as they, poor dears, are unable to make the complex series of adjustments necessary for peaceful and non-violent acceptance of someone, who, due to a complex series of sincerely held and deeply felt beliefs, they regard as a bleeding wog.

TWIGS: Not all. Carm off of it.

BILLY: No. Just the ones he meets.

But GANGE is miles away, studying SAM. Fundamentally he can't like the guy. He couldn't say why, but he feels he's been hard on him.

GANGE: Well O.K. It was Southall if you mus' know. If you mus' know. O.K? Turn you on does it? That makes me anuvver fuckin' statistic dunnit? That was where Evans booked me if you wanner know. Evans an' a good few more. But iss Evans face I remember. Evans face an' Evans size twelve goin' inter my groin like there was no tomorrer. 'E's a plug ugly bastard.

BILLY: And if you really imagine that they'll send you the plug ugly bastard then you are well and truly up a gum tree old chap.

GANGE: Well you wasn't there was you

you useless get? I never noticed you there. I dunno where you fit in I'm sure.

BILLY: I'm sure.

GANGE: You were in ver fuckin' L.S.E. library or wherever you solve the problems of the fuckin' world.

BILLY: This is correct. The London School of Economics ladies and gentlemen. I am often to be seen bowed over a work of sociology, solving a difficult problem in the Labour Theory of Value. I am working on an equation which, when read aloud, will cause the cities of the world to crumble and the poor of the earth to be clad in silver and gold.

TWIGS: Less 'ear it then clever clogs.

BILLY: $X + Y + Z = \$7.765.$

TWIGS: Great.

BILLY: Listen though. Listen. Out there stockbrokers might be dying in the streets. We could be springing into the land of Cockayne.

GANGE: Yore a fuckin' chancer yoo are.

BILLY: My Lord Judge I should point out that my learned friend does not approve of intellectuals. He only approves of me because he met me in a pub. He found out I was an intellectual later. So if you plan to gain his confidence, discuss the Commission for Racial Equality and God knows what else with him then I am afraid you are wasting your time because he won't trust you any more than you trust him. You will have to go through me my Lord.

GANGE: Look –

BILLY: Ah am runnin' dis ship. Ich bin boss of this fucking trial and let me tell you this. Justice is blindfold for a very good reason. It is to hide her red-rimmed, ferrety little eyes. She is looking for someone and it doesn't matter who because as far as I'm concerned it isn't *one* policeman – who my God probably had a bust up with his girlfriend or was only obeying orders or was, indeed provoked – it is so many things – the time the nature of the time, the –

GANGE: SHUT UP CANCHER?

BILLY: WELL WHY ARE YOU BOTHERING ABOUT ONE POOR BASTARD OUTSIDE WHEN WE'VE GOT ONE POOR BASTARD HERE EH? WON'T HE DO JUST AS WELL EH? HE'S THE RIGHT COLOUR HE'S WEARING A UNIFORM HE SEEMS TO HAVE NO IDEAS ABOUT ANYTHING. WON'T HE DO JUST AS WELL AS YOUR FUCKING EVANS EH? WHAT MAKES YOU THINK ONE IS DIFFERENT FROM ANOTHER! IT'S JUST LIKE PICKING CHICKENS OFF A FUCKING RACK! THEY ALL LOOK THE SAME TO ME!

SAM: Isn't that what they say about you?

GANGE: SHUT UP THE BOF A' YER! (*He goes to the door.*) LISSEN YOU LOT! I MEAN IT! I WAN' EVANS! AN' I WAN' 'IM DAHN 'ERE SHARPISH O.K? OR SOMEONE GETS 'URT!

Someone talks back to him.

Wot? Wot?

He can't hear. He slams the door.

Can' 'ear a fuckin' word. Bleed'n waste a' time.

TWIGS: They do that ter gech yer aht in the 'all. Then wham bang.

JANE: Never.

TWIGS: Honest.

JANE: I 'ate coppers.

SAM: Me too.

JOHN: Oh me too.

GANGE: Fuck off you.

BILLY: Shall we proceed?

SAM: I don't think your friend is very interested.

GANGE: AN' YOU FUCK OFF AN' ALL! I'LL TELL YOU WHEN I AM AN' WHEN I AM NOT INCHRESTED! BLIMEY! WOCH YOO FINK YOO ARE GIPSY ROSE LEE?

Moving back into the room.

Less get on wiv it.

BILLY *bows at* SAM.

You. Fatso.

BILLY: Ah. A character witness.

GANGE: An' I tolj yoo ter shuch yer face an' all.

BILLY: To testify for the accused.

GANGE: Testify nuffink. I wish to 'ave words wiv' 'er.

BILLY: In a courtroom that comes to the same thing.

GANGE: 'Oo said anyfink abaht a fuckin' courtroom eh? Except you an' yore fuckin' schoopid games.

BILLY: Try it. (*Pause.*) Ask her a damn question. Speak to her. Try it.

GANGE: Lissen –

BILLY: And don't tell *me* I play games.

GANGE *crosses to her, self-conscious under the attention of the rest of them in a way in which* BILLY, *the natural actor, is not.*

GANGE: 'Ullo.

TWIGS: 'Ullo.

GANGE: We-el.

BILLY: Prosecuting counsel is putting the witness at her ease.

GANGE: Now. Woss yore name?

TWIGS: Twigs.

GANGE: Funny name.

TWIGS: Innit?

BILLY: Objection. I cannot see where this line of questioning is getting us.

SAM: It's called – having a conversation.

BILLY: 'Having a conversation.' 'Having a conversation.' Nobody just 'has a conversation.' They talk to a very particular purpose. They always have something in mind. They want something. Maybe they just want to be *seen* to be talking. Maybe they want to prove that they are a jolly old human being like you and me sahib even if they are carrying a loaded gun and there are a couple of hundred policemen outside and one of them is attempting to add a little tone or dignity to proceedings that would be otherwise squalidly criminal indeed the said two men have entered the premises with the intent of removing large amounts of what is popularly known as money, rather than formulating a series of coherent political demands such as the

immediate euthanasia of Michael Heseltine, the unaesthetised vasectomy of Geoffrey Howe, the twin mastectomy – at sea in comparative darkness – of Margaret Thatcher, the –

GANGE: SHUCH YER FACE! (*Pause.*) An' money weren't all the fuckin' issue as well you know.

BILLY: Yes. The relationship between crime and political oppression is a complex one and –

GANGE: SHUT UP!

But BILLY *has got to him.*
Oh you talk to 'er clever cunt.

BILLY: Your name?

TWIGS: Twigs.

BILLY: Your baptismal name?

TWIGS: Susan Partridge.

BILLY: Age?

TWIGS: Sixteen.

BILLY: Occupation?

TWIGS: Shop assistant.

BILLY: Relationship with the defendant?

TWIGS: Uh?

BILLY: Him. Do you know him?

TWIGS: 'Course I do. 'E's ver fuckin' Security Guard 'ere 'en 'e?

BILLY: Now Miss Partridge – may I ask you if you remember what *you* were doing on October the thirteenth last?

TWIGS: I was 'ere wan' I?

BILLY: And what were you doing?

TWIGS: Woch yoo fink I was doin'? I was sellin' fuckin' tights wasn't I?

BILLY: Lady and lady of the jury we are coming on to dangerous ground here, and at any moment I may, in my capacity of judge prosecutor, decide to alter the rules of the court – what I mean to say members of the jury, witnesses and potential victims, *is* that this court regards ignorance as a very serious matter and if you didn't fucking *know* where the defendant was on October the thirteenth last then you fucking well should have done you see because as far as I am concerned nobody who 'doesn't know' or 'has an alibi' is safe and that goes for members of the jury too doncher know.

TWIGS: Look you. Me an' Jane was 'ere. O.K?

JANE: On ver counter. Sellin' fuckin' tights. O.K?

BILLY: Selling tights is no excuse. Selling tights isn't going to save anybody's soul.

TWIGS: Iss fuckin' borin' an' all.

BILLY: You see – once again we are talking to a witness accused who doesn't seem to care about what he or she was doing on October the thirteenth last year or indeed what anyone was doing to anyone else on the occasion in question which seems to me a very serious crime indeed.

TWIGS: Are you against Woolworf's?

GANGE: We are totally opposed to Woolworf's in all its forms. Especially ver tights counter. We reckon ver tights counter should be jus' ripped off don't we?

TWIGS: Well. Charmin'.

GANGE: An' we are all very anti ve overalls.

JANE: Well. I'm not keen.

TWIGS: Woolworf's is a big con in my opinion.

BILLY: Ah. And why is that?

TWIGS: Well. Look at it this way. At Superdrug we all 'ad a go on arrangin', or ver till as it might be. I mean it was turns right? There was a nice atmosphere wan't there. I mean you 'aj yer locker bucher never used it. Never needed to. But dahn 'ere – iss bitch bitch know wot I mean? Iss not a nice atmosphere.

BILLY: Well that makes pretty exciting listening. That makes us all sit up and beg. As an analysis of a large, multi-national company that suppresses the wages of its employees, maximises profits, outlaws unions and generally behaves like some retail incarnation of Attila the Hun that really scorches the earth doesn't it? And let me tell you that as well as ignorance being no excuse and absence being no excuse this court is certainly not going to toy around with some phoney notion of . . . simplicity or some such load of old baloney in fact we think simplicity is the

great enemy of my Brinjal Bhaji yes oh my spicy Dal and Paratha it is old bean.

GANGE: SHUCHER FACE!

BILLY: NO SHUT YOURS! AND WORK OUT WHO HAS OR HAS NOT THE BOTTLE OR STOMACH OR GUTS TO GO THROUGH WITH THIS EH? IN SPITE OF A CERTAIN PERSON'S BOASTING EH? I'LL TELL YOU I'M ALL RIGHT! MY CONSCIENCE IS CLEAR! I KNOW WHAT I HAVE TO DO! DON'T WORRY ABOUT ME WHEN YOU'RE MAKING EYES AT OUR TWO LOCAL LOVELIES!

TWIGS: 'Ark at 'im!

JANE: Fancies us!

This age and type of girl really gets to BILLY.

BILLY: STOP THAT! STOP THAT! STOP THAT AT ONCE YOU HEAR ME?

GANGE *goes to him, touched by his sudden vulnerability.*

GANGE: Look . . . (*Pause.*) Look don' less quarrel O.K? I . . . (*Pause.*) Look yore O.K. I . . .

SAM: So is he your boyfriend then?

GANGE: SHUCHER FACE YOU SMART ALEC SOD! SHUCHER CLEVER CUNT FACE CANCHER?

SAM: I'm sorry I . . .

GANGE: YOU WOT?

SAM: I just want to . . .

GANGE: TER WOT??

SAM: To understand.

GANGE *crosses to him.*

GANGE: Well understand this arse'ole. I was in one a' yore courts an' I use the word 'your' advisedly – I was in one a' yore magistrate's courts in a well known suburb a London uvverwise known as Barnet – an' the p'lice officer I 'ave mentioned swore deaf an' dumb an' blind that I 'ad belted 'is 'ead against a brick wall. Now ver fact that I coun't punch a paper bag an' this copper is four times my fuckin' size is irrelevant. Wot counts is I done six months inside fer nuffink. Fer fuck all. An' all 'cos some lyin' copper bastard fancied sendin' me dahn. An' I don' notice universal outrage on my be'alf. An' I don' notice people fallin' over theirselves ter give us a job an' ter chreat my p'lice record as jus' one a' them fings that 'appens when you got 'alf the fuckin' Met bent. I 'ave not noticed this occurrin' since my release from the 'Oliday Camp where I was confined courtesy a' the 'Ome Secretary. So you see as far as I'm concerned I'm past understandin' from the likes a' you becos I need a lit'l more than that as of now an' I'm afraid that it on'y takes one look ach yoo ter clock thach yore the type that specialises in nuffink else than that well I don' want no understandin' sonny I tolj yer I'm past understandin' I'm through wiv it I'm all washed up wiv it I want some action sailor boy an' I want it right fuckin' now. I want Evans 'ere. On the line. Eyeball ter bleedin' eyeball. So understand that.

BILLY: And whether they send him or they don't send him it doesn't matter because if we don't have Evans on the line we'll have Karl Malden over there and –

GANGE: LEAVE OFF OF THAT WILLYER?

BILLY: I WILL NOT LEAVE OFF OF THAT! I'VE TOLD YOU WE DON'T WANT AN EYE FOR AN EYE ANY MORE! NOT A TOOTH FOR A TOOTH NEITHER! WE WANT IT FOR A LOT MORE THAN ONE LOUSY POLICEMAN WE WANT IT FOR 'OH BY GOLLY GOSH!' AND 'SEND THEM BACK ON THE BANANA BOAT' AND THE CONSERVATIVE CABINET OH AND WHILE WE'RE AT IT THERE ARE A FEW HIGHLY RESPECTED MEMBERS OF THE INDIAN CIVIL SERVICE THAT WAS I WOULDN'T MIND SEEKING STAKED OUT ON HENDON AERODROME WHILE THE ODD POLO STICK IS HAMMERED THROUGH THEM!

GANGE: We –

BILLY: WE WANT AN ARM AND A HEAD FOR A TOOTH AND A WHOLE FUCKING CARCASE FOR AN EYE OH MY GOLLY GOSH WE WANT SO MANY CARCASES WE ARE A LITTLE BIT BEHIND YOU UNDERSTAND THAT AND WE HAVE DECIDED IT IS TIME TO START EVENING UP WE WANT JUSTICE AND SINCE THEY WON'T GIVE US JUSTICE WE WILL HAVE TO TAKE IT!

GANGE: But don't push it eh? Don't push it too far.

SAM: Look –

GANGE: SHUT UP! SHUT UP! SHUT UP!

TWIGS: You gonner shoot us.

BILLY: WELL WE'VE GOT TO SHOOT SOMEBODY AND THAT'S A FACT!

A voice outside.

VOICE: Can you hear us? Can you hear us?

Everyone freezes.

BILLY: Get to the door.

GANGE *crosses, calls up.*

GANGE: Yeah?

VOICE: There's somebody coming down! He's not armed. O.K?

GANGE: Are you sendin' us Evans?

VOICE: He's not armed. O.K?

We hear footsteps outside. GANGE yanks back the door and there in the doorway is a very young police officer, SMILER. He is wearing bobby-on-the-street gear. He stands in the doorway. Nobody moves.

BILLY: Well what are you waiting for? (*Pause.*) Shoot. Shoot. (*Pause.*) Shoot.

GANGE: BASTARDS! DOUBLE CROSSING COPPER BASTARDS!

Act Two

The same as before. The same instant. SMILER *moves a little into the room.*

SMILER: Is this your bicycle sir? The rear light is not on. You 'ave to 'ave a rear light you know.

BILLY: Lost your nerve?

GANGE: This isn't fuckin' Evans you git.

(*Moving past him to the door. He shouts up.*) NO-ONE GOES FROM 'ERE TILL YOU SEND ME EVANS RIGHT? I DON' WANT NO PERFORMIN' SEA-LION FRESH FROM POLICE 'O' LEVEL WIV 'IS MUM STITCHED 'IS NAME INTER 'IS UNIFORM! I WANT FUCKIN' EVANS!

BILLY: And now they're winning. You let them get away with this they're winning. Shoot. Shoot. Shoot.

GANGE: OH SHUCHER FACE YOU! YORE ANUVVER EXPERT AINCHER?

SMILER: Evans didn't fancy it. They're talkin' to 'im.

BILLY: Surprise surprise.

SMILER: 'E's S.P.G.

JANE: Woss S.P.G?

BILLY: It stands for Strangle Proletarian Golliwogs. It is a highly trained, mobile, disciplinary unit, of highly trained, mobile, disciplined gorillas. They swing from lamp post to lamp post and when they see a person of Asian origin they land on his head. Shoot. Time is running out. Shoot.

GANGE: Ah leave it aht.

SMILER: I said if you wanted a copper you could 'ave me.

GANGE: SHIT!

He kicks the door shut.

BILLY: You have no understanding of what is going on here. You are quite obviously simple-minded. I suggest your unhealthy desire to be locked up with a couple of deranged psychopaths is part of the Judaeo-Christian assumption that one person can accumulate in himself all the wrong, suffering, tears, pain, howling etc. etc. and by substituting himself somehow redeem or make bearable the nasty little slag heap on which we poor mortals perform well let me tell you P.C.49 you ain't up there you are down here and you have walked into a courtroom and it ain't no ordinary courtroom what you walked into this am a people's courtroom, a packing room courtroom an' we do it de people's way brudder we know that there is no hope

and redemption that there is only years of wrong and suffering and yes sahib and no sahib and the punishment will start at any place and will go on for centuries and we still won't be even and if my learned friend will not despatch you out of hand then you can shut up and watch us do the same favour for your uniformed friend over there.

TWIGS: 'E fuckin' means it. 'E's goin' ter –

JANE: Look John ain't done nuffink. 'E isn't even –

SAM moves to GANGE.

SAM: Seriously. Don't you think we could stop this? Before it gets serious?

GANGE: Serious? Serious? This 'as jus' got totally an' completely fuckin' ridiculous. This 'as just gorn badly off of the rails. (*Kicking the door and laughing hysterically.*) Oh blimey. Oh fuck me. Oh stop it Eric.

SMILER: Look. You wan'ed a copper. I'm a copper 'en I?

GANGE: Oh you ain' a copper. Yore a fuckin' Christmas present you are.

SMILER: I am a policeman. O.K?

GANGE: Woch yoo do then son? Stand in Piccadilly Circus an' tell people the way ter the Tower a' London? Pose fer fuckin' American tourists ahtside a' Buckingham Palace? You ain' a policeman my son. You are a cake decoration you are.

BILLY: Are you going to insult him instead of shooting him? Do you think that will be an acceptable substitute?

BILLY goes on to taunt him in Punjabi. GANGE answers him in English.

GANGE: I'll shoot oo I like cunt. An' remember – I bought ver fuckin' gun din't I?

BILLY: So what do you propose to do with him?

GANGE goes to the door.

GANGE: YOU CAN 'AVE P.C. 49 BACK! I DON'T FANCY 'IM! O.K? 'E ADDS NUFFING TER THE PROCEEDIN'S!

SMILER: They was worried you was goin' ter do sunnink to 'im. (*Indicates JOHN.*)

BILLY: Are they recording us for posterity then?

SMILER: They got mikes. Dahn ver ventilator. Everywhere.

GANGE: 'ULLO COPPER! 'OW'S YORE EARS?

SMILER: They was gettin' worried.

GANGE: An' on account John Wayne wasn't feelin' too well they sent you.

BILLY: Can we get on?

GANGE: Fuck off you. I'm talkin' to my noo friend.

BILLY: Having decided to insult him rather than shoot him you have now made the logical progression to being jolly good friends with him. I say old boy – (*Parody Indian waiter voice.*) are you going to end up applying for the uniform yourself? Are you going to become the second Asian policeman in Great Britain? Are you going to be a jolly old community policeman and be photographed by the Bradford Evening Telegraph but otherwise kept clear of anything more significant than multi-racial primary schools?

SAM: What's wrong with multi-racial primary schools?

BILLY: Ah. If life stopped after the eleven plus what a wunnerful world this would be.

GANGE: Shucher face an' let me talk ter my noo friend.

BILLY: The dignity of the court is compromised.

GANGE: Iss the judge's job 'e's after. (*To* SMILER.) So yore notion is – we let this lot fuck off an' yoo stay dahn 'ere wivus.

SMILER: Thass it.

GANGE: Don' fancy it. They wouldn't kick up abaht us shootin' you. Yore obviously an inessential component of the p'lice force.

SMILER: All right all right. So wot if I ain't six foot five.

TWIGS: More like two foot free you are.

SMILER: Give over give over.

JOHN: 'Ow tall are you actually?

BILLY: LADIES AND GENTLEMEN PLEASE! CAN WE DISCUSS SOMETHING A LITTLE MORE URGENT THAN THE HEIGHT OF A POLICEMAN PLEASE? CAN WE –

SMILER: The height of a policeman is very important.

BILLY *turns on* GANGE *and shouts at him in Punjabi. But* GANGE *is enjoying the absurdity of the threat to* BILLY. *He smiles, waves his gun.*

GANGE: Carry on carry on.

SMILER: Well ter me a p'liceman should be big right? I mean there yoo are an' 'ardened criminal right? An' there's this lit'l midget p'liceman lookin' up ach yer going' "ello 'ello 'ello!' in an' 'igh squeaky voice. Well. Iss not on is it? You 'it 'im doncher? An' I'm not the kind a short person oo looks people fairly an' squarely in the belly button an' sez "Ow are you?" in a big tough voice. I'm ashamed a' bein' a short person.

JOHN: I'm five seven. In me socks.

SMILER: I'd like ter be a basket ball player I would.

BILLY: FOR GOD'S SAKE CAN WE SHUT THIS PERSON UP PLEASE! I DON'T WISH TO HEAR ABOUT HIS AMBITION TO BE A BASKETBALL PLAYER.

GANGE: Well I do. An' I got the shooter.

TWIGS: Yoo 'av ter be five foot four ter get in the p'lice force doncher?

JOHN: Thass it.

SMILER: Well I've five foot four.

GANGE: Never.

SMILER: I am. I fuckin' am.

GANGE: No way are you five foot four.

SMILER: I fuckin' am.

BILLY: Listen –

TWIGS: I'd say you was nearer five one.

SMILER: I AM FIVE FOOT FOUR! (*Pause.*) Almost.

GANGE: Ah ha! Ah ha! Almost! This is it. Almost but not quite. I mean this is wot I am chryin' ter tell you son. You can be five foot three and seventy-nine eightieths of an inch an' yoo still ain't five foot four. You still ain't a regular, officially approved British Bobby. I mean I on'y 'ave ter look ach yer ter know that you are nuffink but a mug. Which is why no way do I intend to accept you as a short or long term substitute for my friend Evans.

SMILER: All I'm sayin' is that –

BILLY: So what *are* you going to do with him?

SMILER: All I'm sayin' is – thach yoo got a grievance. I mean it may be a legitimate grievance. But it ain't ter do wiv 'im is it? It –

BILLY: Well?

GANGE: I fink 'e makes a lovely counsel fer the defence.

BILLY: LISTEN THEY AREN'T GOING TO SEND YOU EVANS O.K? *THIS* IS IT! THIS!

Indicating the room.

What is happening here. This is it. This is the justice you are going to get. There isn't any other kind of justice except down here. This is it here and now. And if you've decided that you don't want it, that you want to have pity where they would not and will not have pity that is your affair but don't come whining to me about it when they take you out of here and off in their big black vans and someone less amusing than our friend here kicks you round a cell O.K? You went out to get it with a gun in your hand didn't you? Didn't I tell you all about that? Didn't I tell you what we would do with the money and how we would act and didn't you believe me? (*Close to him. Affectionate.*) But now you have it you don't like it. You shrink from this justice that you were so sure that you wanted. You think it's foolish or shameful or irrelevant or lacking in something. Yes yes yes. You are afraid of what we are doing here. You don't think we have a right to try the guilty, to make laws. It seems so pitiful doesn't it? What do you want to do with it? Decorate it as they do? Conceal it in adequate clothes? No. This is it.

To the rest of them. When he's up like this you could believe that the gun in his hand is real.

AND MAKE SURE THAT YOU UNDERSTAND THAT O.K?

(*To* GANGE:) The law does not allow for late evidence O.K? I don't wish to hear about the damn nice bobbies. I am sure there are hundreds of damn nice bobbies all over the place. I am sure the Cotswolds are stuffed full of damn nice bobbies with nothing to do all day but pat tourists on the head and tell dogs what time it is. But we are not talking about the damn nice bobbies we are talking about the nasty ones. And we can't afford to make any mistakes. You select your target and then you –

GANGE: A laugh.

BILLY: Uh?

GANGE: A laugh. For. A. Laugh.

Pause.

'Ow come yoo always know woch yore gonner do next eh? Yore so well prepared. I ain't so well prepared. I dunno wot I might do next. I might shoot ver lot a' yer. I dunno.

BILLY: What we said was –

GANGE: I forgotten what we said. I can't remember. And did it signify? We was pissed most a' the time weren't we? You wanner sew it all up before it's started. An' 'alf a' this stuff yoo come out with –

BILLY: Is a little complicated for you? You don' understand it? It bothers you?

GANGE: SHUCHER FACE!

He relapses into a brief, wounded sulk.

TWIGS: Did you know each uvver over there?

BILLY: The girl wants to know if we knew each other over there. Well I think I can answer that fairly clearly. Coming as we quite clearly do from the same mud hut in the same monsoon-racked village of Lahore or Djapati or wherever it is it is quite clear that not only did we know each other 'over there' – we shared the same bowl of fluffy rice, we worshipped the same damn cow, we posed for the same fucking Oxfam advert we were as thick as thieves 'over there'.

Close to her.

A. the Indian sub-continent is a little bit bigger and more complicated than the Woolworth's staff canteen and B. as far as he is concerned there isn't an 'over there'.

Because he happens to be a British citizen born here educated here. 'Over there' is Isleworth as far as he's concerned. Oh and C. as far as he and I are concerned 'knowing' each other was a series of curious and unsatisfactory drinks in places with wild romantic names like 'The Sun In Splendour' 'The Hole in the Wall' and other venues where I am to be found nightly, polishing my equations and spinning tighter and tighter webs for people like you.

SAM: You're drinking friends?

GANGE: I won't say we was friends wouldjer? I'd say we jrink tergevver.

SAM: I mean were your families close?

GANGE: Nosey sod. We don' 'ave no fuckin' fam'lies O.K? We're full-time orphans we are. The bof of us.

SMILER: Tell you wot. Why doncher let the girls go?

GANGE: I toljer. Counsel. For. The. Defence.

BILLY: I am afraid my learned friend that they are needed for the trial.

He paces. The actor in him can't resist this.

Citizens on the electoral roll may as presently constituted be required to serve as jurors and to act as accomplices after the fact. They may also be required to serve as judge, magistrates, ushers, stenographers, tables, chairs, stationery and other things needful for the dispensal of justice in this, the first really truly and democratically devised legal system in the West, the packing room code or the Woolworth's Statutes, Hounslow MDXIXVIII ii.2. paragraph four section three 'no-one shall leave until Billy says'.

SMILER: Now lissen –

GANGE is behind him and trundling him into position on an exact and opposite spot to BILLY's.

GANGE: Defence counsel. Iss a lovely job. They don' 'ang defence counsels. Iss a nice safe job. You stand up. You make all ver right noises. You stick up fer 'umanity. An' when they 'ang yore client, you say 'Oh well. Fuck it. Win one. Lose one'. An' yoo go 'ome fer a couple a' Martinis. Iss a good job is defence counsel. Stand there. (*Turns and crosses*

to the door.) I CAN 'EAR YOU! WOCH YOO TAKE US FOR EH? LIKE LIT'L MICE AHT THERE! I CAN 'EAR YOU! WOCH YOU UP TO? NAH LISSEN I GOT ONE FINAL AND ULTIMATE DEMAND AND THAT IS FER EVANS O.K? AN' IF 'E AIN'T DAHN 'ERE SOON SOMEONE'S GOIN' TER GET 'URT ALL RIGHT?

BILLY: DECENTLY AND LEGALLY AND OFFICIALLY HURT O.K?

GANGE: Now you'll need a witness fer the defence woncher?

SAM: Me?

TWIGS: Yore the judge you are.

SAM: So?

TWIGS: Oo's the judge if yore a witness?

SMILER: I'll be the judge.

GANGE: Steady on son. This isn't Monopoly you know. Don' blow it. Steady. Steady.

BILLY: Listen –

GANGE: She can be the judge.

BILLY: Listen –

GANGE: SHUT UP! I SAID SHE COULD BE THE JUDGE! O.K? I FINK SHE'S WELL QUALIFIED! I FINK SHE COULD BE A VERY GOOD JUDGE! SHE SHOWS APTITUDE IN MY OPINION! LOOK AT 'ER! EH?

TWIGS: Charmed I'm sure.

JANE: Woss she 'ave ter do?

BILLY: She has to obey my young friend. Having accused me of being the bossy type, he is showing some signs of –

GANGE: GIVE OVER!

But there's some truth in this. To cope with his frustration and confusion GANGE is becoming much more of the boss figure.

She 'as ter be in charge.

TWIGS: Blimey.

GANGE: See? A nach'ral leader.

BILLY: We will hear the witness.

SAM: I thought she was in charge!

BILLY (*trying to win back ground from GANGE*): MOVE!

SAM *moves.*

Now. State your name.

SMILER: Objection.

BILLY: Please be quiet.

GANGE: Objection sustained.

BILLY: I thought she was the damn judge old bean.

GANGE: 'Oi – you wiv ver big tits – say 'Objection sustained'.

TWIGS: Objection sustained.

GANGE: There. Good judge en't she?

SAM: Oh the only good judge is one in your pocket.

GANGE: FUCK OFF YOU YOU RUDE KNOW-ALL CUNT! YORE A WITNESS YOU ARE! NOW YOU GIVE EVIDENCE WHILE WE'RE WAITING! LESS 'AVE A LIT'L LESS A' YORE OPINIONS! I'VE 'AD ENOUGH A' PEOPLE WIV OPINIONS!

BILLY: What is the nature of the objection?

SMILER: None a' yore business.

BILLY: What isn't my business?

SMILER: 'Is name.

GANGE: Now lissen son. When I said you was defence counsel I wan'ed you ter take me seriously. But not *that* seriously. I mean there are rules yer know. We're all in this tergevver you know. Less 'ave a bit a' co-operation. Carry on my learned friend.

BILLY: Oh I wish I'd got a different gun. (*Snaps into his legal manner.*) Name?

SAM: Samuel Sherlock.

BILLY: Profession?

SAM: Student.

BILLY: Place of study?

SAM: The London School of Economics.

A nasty pause.

BILLY: Now just a *moment* . . .

GANGE: Trickee!

BILLY: Am I to understand that you are a member of my dear old Alma Mater?

SAM: You are.

BILLY: I must say – I find that rather hard to believe. (*Pacing.*) You see – you don't look to me in any way like a student at the London School of Economics. And you don't sound like one in any way whatsoever. And I am a bit of an expert at spotting people from the London School of Economics. I can spot one at four hundred yards. My God I know when one of them is behind me in a cinema queue. I can sense when they're in the neighbour-hood. Good gracious me I know a student of the London School of Economics, from, say, a museum curator or a zoo-keeper or a part-time gardener, or, shall we say, an unemployed Pakistani actor good golly gosh yes. Because I'm an old student of the school doncher know? I'm an alumnus. Yes. You've probably seen me in the North Library working on my equation.

SAM: I can't remember having seen you there.

BILLY: Objection – the witness is questioning my cross-examination.

SAM: No no – I am cross-examining your question.

GANGE: FUCK OFF CLEVER CUNT! GET ON WIV IT!

BILLY: He doesn't like you.

GANGE: An' yoo like 'im doncher? Went ter school tergevver dincher?

TWIGS: 'Ere –

GANGE: The judge speaks.

TWIGS: Never mind.

JOHN: Can I sit down? I'm getting tired.

BILLY: Listen young man – you'll sit down when your trial is over and not before.

JOHN: Give us a break.

GANGE: Sit dahn.

BILLY: It's clear to me that the witness is lying.

TWIGS: Oh yeah?

SAM: When did you say you were there?

BILLY: 10.30 to 3.00 and 5.30 to 11 o' clock.

GANGE: Except on Sundays. Twelve ter two an' seven to ten-firty.

BILLY: I ask you – is that any way to run a library. The thirst for knowledge goes unsatisfied at weekends. (*Pacing.*) I think the witness is quite clearly an alcoholic, a parasite, a drifter and a teller of tall stories. If you seriously expect the court to believe that you, a student at the so-called London School of Economics, could actually find yourself in Woolworth's in Hounslow at five o'clock purchasing a pair of tights, and, further-more, consequent on the purchase of the said tights, to allow yourself, in company with these people to be herded into the basement of the said Woolworth's and allow nay permit yourself not only to adopt the role and function of 'judge' but then, willy-nilly, to abandon that role and become a 'defence witness' in a sort of 'trial' well I am afraid Mr. Sherlock that as something of an expert in the ways of the world all this strikes me as a little bit less than plausible, *especially in view* of the fact that you are claiming to be a student of the very institute of higher education that I myself attended. Come Mr. Sherlock – what next? War crimes in Cambodia? Bad weather in June? What next will we be required to swallow?

SMILER: May I cross-examine?

GANGE: When 'e's finished.

BILLY: Now Mr. Sherlock – I want you to tell me where you were on the afternoon of October thirteenth last?

SMILER: Why?

GANGE: You're a bit late you are son.

BILLY: I really think you should have briefed your lawyer more carefully Mr. Latham.

JOHN: Look I've 'ad –

SAM: I was in the library of the London School of Economics.

BILLY: Well well well.

Strolling across to him, thumbs in his lapels.

When you hang you'll hang together. As my young friend is being sentenced – as he appears in the dock, it seems you have all devised cunningly constructed alibis. One of you is 'selling tights' another posing as a 'student' at the 'London School of Economics' presumably on the day when the alleged offence is supposed to have occurred but didn't that is to say the soi-disant 'riot' at Southall you were all at home having a cup of tea eh Mr. Latham?

JOHN: I dunno woch yore on abaht. I toljer I don't read ver paprs.

BILLY *has turned on him.*

BILLY: Oh perhaps you never even *knew* that the National Front was allowed to hold a meeting right in the heart of one of the largest Asian communities in this country? Perhaps that has escaped your notice?

SAM: Look – he –

BILLY: Or perhaps the accused hasn't heard of the National Front? Perhaps he is unaware that they are allowed to prance up and down and suggest the forcible export of large numbers of men women and children in the interests of free speech? Perhaps he thinks they are a Zambian liberation movement? Or perhaps he doesn't 'think' at all?

JOHN: I've 'eard a' them. They're . . . a . . . party . . . they . . . er . . .

BILLY: It seems to me you see gentlemen that here we are dealing with a highly organised conspiracy going back at least two thousand years and involving literally millions of people.

SAM: So you take a principled objection to the concept of innocence?

GANGE: Turn it up fuckface. Answer 'is question right?

BILLY: All the white men are guilty sahib. They took my cow and they took my land and they won't give me their Shreddies or their Puffa Puffa rice. (*But he is caught by* SAM. *He finds* SAM *as interesting as* GANGE *finds him infuriating. Moving back to him.*) Innocence is all very well. But where does it begin?

TWIGS: In child'ood.

GANGE: 'E likes 'im. 'E fuckin' loves 'im.

SAM: It's nice for him to have someone to talk to.

BILLY: It must be because we're old graduates doncher know?

GANGE: Yore a graduate a' caterin' you are. University a' bleed'n take away meals thass you.

SAM: No I'm sorry. But it interests me. I mean –

GANGE: Shut up!

SAM: Why this?

GANGE: Give over!

SAM: Why though?

GANGE: Oo's askin' ver questions 'ere?

BILLY: HE IS, O.K?

SAM: It isn't a very organised protest is it?

BILLY *moves close to him.*

BILLY: Well my young friend and I are not very organised people. Why does bloody everyone have to be organised? We don't approve of organisations. We like the gesture you see. The beautiful gesture that lights up the sky. We are not at all typical. We abhor the typical.

SAM: Terrorism.

BILLY: Do we look like terrorists?

SAM: No no no. You look like students from the London School of Economics. (BILLY *slaps him.*) That's a real woman's trick.

BILLY: SHUT UP!

GANGE: Well lissen ter me than cancher? Once you start lettin' 'im arst the questions. Oo's in charge 'ere eh? Oo's in danger a' losin' enfusiasm? Proceed. Get on wiv it. Start. Attack. O.K?

And now GANGE is winding BILLY up for the attack.

BILLY: I take it then Mr. Sherlock that you were unaware of the events –

GANGE *has gone to the door.*

GANGE: EVANS! EVANS OR WE SHOOT YORE FUCKIN' USELESS SECURITY GUARD O.K?

JOHN: Lissen –

GANGE: SHUT UP! O.K? (*Moving back to where he thinks the mikes might be.*) WE'RE RUNNIN' AHT A PATIENCE O.K?

BILLY: Which is what they want. (*Back in control now.*) We understand that your defence would appear to be that no-one has to be in two places at the same time that is to say, as Voltaire has so ably pointed out in French Versus the Rest of the World, we all have a jardin and if we cultivate it, well, it isn't our fault if they're killing dogs in the street in fact as long as they don't throw 'em over our jolly old fence that is just bung ho by us.

SAM: I wouldn't describe that as my defence at all.

GANGE: Oh you piss me off you do.

SAM (*rapidly*): Being a student of the London School of Economics you see I know there is a place for protest and that there are channels that can be followed that is to say the structure or infra-structure provided by the labour movements, the movements of the Third World countries, what could be fancifully described as the dispossessed of the world, but that these channels as I said must be gone through i.e. experienced and indeed will and must lead to violent confrontation although that violent confrontation will not *necessarily* occur in the basement of Woolworth's in –

GANGE: Well where will it occur then Chrotsky? Eh? In the Dominion, Leicester Square or wot? 'Ow come you know so much abaht vis confrontation anyway? Wot makes you the fuckin' expert? Eh?

SAM (*still fast, needling* BILLY): Having studied the ins and outs of various kinds of revolution and protest and having observed quietly to myself the similarity between your unplanned and badly co-ordinated act of aggression and that of, say, the Social Revolutionaries in pre-Revolutionary Russia I think I can confidently assert that although up to now I have 'held my tongue' (all right? good enough for you?) and made an attempt to 'understand' you I must take this opportunity of saying that there are organisations which are legitimate and useful and do not mean your being classified with crooks, drunks and thieves. I am referring to –

GANGE: SHUT UP OR I WILL FUCKIN' SHOOCH YER I SWEAR I WILL! (*Pause.*) If there's one thing I cannot stand and that is people wiv answers to everyfing. Yore like my ol' man you are.

But SAM pushes on, out-parodying BILLY now. Directing his speech at him, fast, mechanical, relentless.

SAM: Furthermore I think you will find any number of people who are only too willing, after the event, to discuss with any amount of sympathy the fact that you are symptoms of something that should and surely will be corrected i.e. racialism, but I don't think you'll find many people prepared to accept you as a factor of real relevance unless you go ahead and A. shoot somebody or B. recruit as many members as the organisations I have mentioned which are legitimately furthering the interests of your community in spite of the fascist bully-boy tactics of the wreckers and thugs who are –

BILLY: STOP IT! STOP IT! STOP IT!

SAM: What's the matter? Don't you like what you are? Or is it what you do that troubles you?

BILLY: At the moment it is *you* that troubles me Mr. Sherlock. I'm afraid that, fond as I am of the rational I've always . . . (*Winding down.*) I've always . . . (*And the two nearly grin at each other, professionals amused by each other.*) You are a very *difficult* witness.

SAM: I'm all for fighting back.

BILLY: Are you acquainted with the defendant Mr. Sherlock?

SAM: I know his type.

BILLY: And do you condone it?

SAM: I think it will vanish away.

BILLY: You don't think there's much call for small security guards.

SAM: I think the petit bourgeois is doomed.

BILLY (*suddenly hectoring*): Well isn't that what I said?

SAM: I think his uniform is quite attractive.

BILLY: You keep making the most unpleasant insinuations Mr. Sherlock. Insinuations of a sexual nature. I wonder whether it is you and not I who are the homo –

SAM: I think there's no harm in him.

BILLY: I don't think you realise the seriousness of the charge Mr. Sherlock. This young man is charged that, on October 13th he did wilfully impersonate P.C. Evans at a magistrate's court in Barnet there lying through his teeth in order to effect the conviction of one young Asian to wit him over there and that on or before that day he did conspire with or do impressions of the Special Patrol Group in order to effect the harassment and embarrassment of the people of Southall and that on earlier occassions he did knowingly cause or conspire incidents at the Grunwick processing factory in North London, India House, the Saltley Gates and sundry other places, there wounding maliciously representatives of legally constituted organisations going about their business in the – (*Pausing.*) Oh and if that sounds pretty bloody stupid old bean – you should have been in fucking Barnet. Because that sounded a whole lot stupider to me. And I had to listen to it. For quite a long time.

SMILER: May I ajress ver court?

GANGE: Good idea.

BILLY: Look –

GANGE: Relax.

BILLY: I really don't understand you. One minute you're mustard keen. The next . . .

GANGE: Wot?

BILLY: I don't know . . . chicken?

GANGE: I'll do wot I 'ave ter do. (*To the mikes.*) GET THAT?

BILLY: Oh I'm sure. It's just that sometimes I get the impression – you don't want us to finish here.

GANGE: Look –

BILLY: Because after we have heard the witnesses we proceed to closing arguments and then we proceed to sentence and I don't know whether you want that you see old man.

GANGE: Never you mind wot I want. I know wot I fuckin' want. (*To SMILER, irritably.*) Get on wiv it you. Go on.

SMILER: May I say first of all that I 'ave not understood a single word of wot 'as bin goin' on 'ere an' I do not wish ter cross-examine this witness on account of I cannot understand a fuckin' word 'e sez. Step down.

BILLY: My learned friend does not want to

hear evidence on the grounds that it may confuse him.

SMILER: Look – (*To* GANGE.) Maybe Evans give evidence against you right? I mean maybe 'e was bendin' it. I don' know. But it ain't so much ter do wiv this lot right?

BILLY: I was afraid he was going to be theoretical.

SMILER: All I'm sayin' is that I know wot iss like. I mean 'e 'ad 'is report ter write din't 'e? I mean iss no joke the Police Force mate. Iss all reports. At 0945 hrs I went inter the Gents and at 0953 I emerged an' . . . you know. I mean when 'e –

BILLY: What do you mean? Are you defending the system of justice under which –

SMILER: Justice justice justice. Woch yoo on abaht justice all the time for eh? We ain't talkin' abaht justice you schoopid cunt we're talkin' abaht a magistrate's court which ain't the same fing at all. Christ I mean nobody's perfect. I mean give us a break I seen villains walk away in my time look *justice* –

BILLY: Is what precisely?

SMILER: Oh look I dunno. Iss a few people in a fuckin' room probably. Iss me an' 'im. Or me an' yoo. Or me an' my ol' man. I mean iss wot we doo innit? Thass all it is. An' as we're 'ere. Jus' the so many of us. I mean . . . wot we do. Wot we do to each uvver eh? (*Pause.*) Look – far as I'm concerned none of us done nuffink O.K? I reckon we are as we are. No argument. I got no preconceived notions. All I'm sayin' is – I come dahn 'ere. I mean – look – if you want sunnink you 'ave me. I can't bear ter fink of it. You take me. No arguments. Jus' sweet an' nach'ral. Like a baby. Baby does this – you do that. Let the sods go. Let that poor lit'l sod off of the 'ook. O.K? All right?

GANGE: 'En 'e sweet?

BILLY: Oh if it were only you and me and him and her. If there were nobody outside the room. Or nothing beyond the city. No sea to confuse the shoreline, no countries beyond what we owned ourselves, no misery complicating our misery, making it less and worse than

it is. Look – you want to be a child. I can see it in your face. But you know far too much. You have a sophisticated little smile. Why. My Golly Gosh I'll tell you what you are . . . you're a sham . . . you're a faux-naïf you're a fake you're not a policeman at all you're a doll you're a model you're an excrescence you're a waste of time you're a trick policeman you're –

He's worked himself up enough to let go now.

YOU'RE A DISGRACE TO YOUR CLOTH! YOU HEAR? THERE'S A WHOLE LOT OUTSIDE THIS ROOM! DON'T FORGET THAT MR. COMMUNITY POLICEMAN! DON'T FORGET THAT THE NEXT TIME YOU PAT A BLACK GIRL ON THE HEAD! (*Close to him.*) THERE ARE WOMEN QUEUEING IN YOUR PORTS TO SEE THEIR HUSBANDS! WOMEN WITH CHILDREN WHO ARE DENIED THE 'SIMPLE AND NACH'RAL RIGHT' TO SEE THEM! THERE ARE FAMILIES SEPARATED! THERE ARE WOMEN MADE STATELESS AND MEN WHO LOSE THEIR FAMILIES TO GRATIFY THE IGNORANT SENSIBILITIES OF PEOPLE LIKE THIS AND THIS AND THIS! THERE IS BUCKETFULS OF IT AND JUST YOU REMEMBER YOU WEAR THE FUCKING UNIFORM OLD BOY! YOU WEAR THE SAME UNIFORM WHY IT COULD BE HIS UNIFORM OR IT COULD BE THE COSTUME WORN BY THOSE *CUNTS* WHO STOOD MY WIFE UP AGAINST A WALL AND –

He stops, totally and eerily calm suddenly.

Look. It's obvious sahib that I'm having you on. Oh so obvious. I probably haven't got a wife any more than you're a real policeman. I'm probably making her up in order to titillate your cheap concern. I'm not the sort of wallah to have a wife. I'm clearly not the marrying kind oh my Golly Gosh no. Oh no by samosa I'm not do you see? I must be lying because it's just too perfect isn't it this man running around with a boy from Southall and his wife is in that shed in Southampton or wherever it is being jumped up and down on by Customs

Officers well that's just too much of a coincidence wouldn't you say? That's entirely unacceptable eh? After all coincidences rarely happen in rooms do they? Or if they happen they happen to suit someone's convenience – to tie in with someone's design, someone who wants someone damaged or killed or . . . (*Switches to parody Indian waiter voice.*) Look it's pretty damn clear to me that I'm not from the Indian sub-continent at all. I'm probably from the B.B.C. Light Entertainment department. I'm probably blacked up you see. I'm an English actor doing a funny voice eh? But hear this – (*In genuine grief.*) The mother of my children and my children are being kept in a big stone shed near Heathrow Airport because there are certain . . . difficulties. So is it any wonder that I imagine the craziest things. That I have this urge to hurt back. That I dream about . . .

SAM: The London School of Economics.

BILLY: SHUT UP MISTER! HOW LONG YOUR PAPERS GOOD FOR EH? WHEN YOU GOING HOME?

SAM: I am home.

BILLY: Ah citizenship. What a glorious thing. Ah waited de whole of de Cibbil War ter get me U.S. citizenship right? Ah can vote now. Mein Gott say vot you like about Hitler he's a mensch he's a German citizen yes? Zees ees eet. To belong somewhere. A leet'l 'ouse in zer country. Zer knowledge zat you are at one weez your fellow man zat you are a part of a country *boyo* learnin' the Welsh language, thinking Welsh thoughts and being, well, du, being pretty bloody . . . Welsh actually. (*In celebration.*) BELONGING BELONGING BELONGING WHAT A THING! TO BELONG TO THIS LOT! TO ACTUALLY BE A FUCKING HUMAN!

SMILER: I ain't got no ties. No kids. Not married. Jus' me. Look – you mean it doncher? You fuckin' mean it you do. Look. I 'ate my job. I ain' no policeman I ain't . . . Christ oo needs it. Look – let the sod go – I –

BILLY: We don't want you I'm afraid. We want the security guard.

SMILER: But *why*?

BILLY: BECAUSE THAT IS THE LAW O.K? GOOD ENOUGH REASON?

SMILER: 'E AIN' EVEN A FUCKIN' COPPER! LOOK 'AVE ME!

GANGE: I thought you wasn't a copper you said.

SMILER: Listen –

BILLY: Prove it. Prove you're a bloody policeman. Go on. Prove you're worth shooting. Go on. Prove it.

SMILER *has been frightened. He is sure now that they mean business.*

This martyrdom business is too much like . . . choice for me. Down here we have only democratically elected martyrs. Only martyrs who have been through the selection procedure. Martyrs who have been on the list. Martyrs who have been trained as martyrs, qualified martyrs, people's martyrs, packing room martyrs.

SMILER: 'Ello 'ello 'ello.

GANGE: You done that already.

SMILER: Watch it sonny.

GANGE: Ye-e es.

TWIGS: 'En 'e good?

SMILER: Are you aware that you were exceeding the speed limit in a built-up area? I must warn you that anything you say may be taken down and may be used in evidence against you. (*Silence.*) I warned the suspect that he was in danger of endangering the lives of passers-by by his actions and he replied 'Fuck off copper'. I then told him that I was about to arrest him whereupon he produced a long iron bar and hit me on the head. I then further cautioned him that he was in danger of assaulting a police officer, whereupon he produced an Armalite rifle and fired twelve rounds into my stomach and chest. I then cautioned him again. (*Silence.*) Lost yer way 'ave you sonny? It's left left and left again. (*Settles back on his feet.*) Lovely evening. Lovely evening. (*Bitter.*) It's those bastards who interfere with little girls. God wouldn't I like to get my 'and on them. I'd kill 'em. I'd strangle 'em. I've always liked little girls. (*Getting desperate.*) 'Ello 'ello 'ello.

GANGE: Now you done that three times.

SMILER: WELL I DIN'T SAY I LIKED

IT DID I? I DIN'T SAY I WAS A PARTICULARLY GOOD POLICEMAN! I DON'T LIKE IT AS A MATTER OF A FACT AND AS A MATTER OF A FACT I AM A BLEED'N AWFUL P'LICEMAN ON ACCOUNT I'M BAD AT GAMES AND I'M ONE MILLIONF OF AN INCH TOO SHORT O.K? BUT I AM A POLICEMAN AN' BEARING' THAT IN MIND I SEEM TO 'AVE MORE TER DO WIV THIS THAN THAT POOR LIT'L SHAKIN' SOD OVER THERE O.K? SO CAN YOU LET 'IM OFF OF THAT 'OOK AN' –

JOHN: Ooo's shakin'?

TWIGS: You are John.

JANE: An' I ain't surprised.

SAM: I tell you – your young friend isn't keen.

GANGE: Don't you be so fuckin' sure abaht that arse'ole. Dinch yoo know? I'm an untypical runaway desperado barmy boots teenage monster in wolf's clothin'. I might do anyfing. You can't rely on me son. An' they ain't lookin' ter send me Evans are they now? (*He goes to the door.*) ARE YOU NOW? NOW YOU KNOW WOCH YORE DOIN'! IT'LL BE ON YORE 'ANDS COPPERS! NOT MINE O.K?

BILLY: We are approaching sentence lady and lady of the jury. We have only one more witness after which we shall proceed to closing arguments and sentence. So you better be good dear. Come back inside.

GANGE: They don' answer. They don' . . .

BILLY: No. I told you. They don't. This is where it happens. Here. Here. Here. Now do you believe me? Eh?

GANGE: Joo know? I fink I fuckin' do. (*He closes the door and walks back.*) Take the stand young lady.

SAM: As judge I would like to say –

BILLY: Are you getting nervous now?

SAM: I –

BILLY: Have you decided I'm more than a big mouth? You can deny my existence if you like. You can cast foul aspersion on my . . . academic qualifications . . . but I tell you . . . I'm going to do it. Oh yes I

am.

JANE: Look –

BILLY: Stand there please.

JANE: 'E's all right is John.

BILLY: The witness is in a hurry to testify. She is impressed by the court.

GANGE: Woss yore name love?

JANE: Jane.

GANGE: Fancy 'im do yer?

BILLY: The cross-examination is now proceeding.

GANGE: Fuck off. Fancy 'im do yer?

JANE: Well I –

TWIGS: She went aht wiv 'im once.

JANE: I never.

TWIGS: She did.

JANE: I never.

TWIGS: She did.

JANE: Well once.

JOHN: Twice.

JANE: O.K. Twice. (*Pause.*) Look 'e's all right. O.K?

BILLY: And why is he 'all right'?

JANE: 'E woun' 'urt a flea.

GANGE: Wot did 'e do then?

JANE: Nuffink.

GANGE: Carm on –

JANE: Nuffink. (*Pause.*) Well 'e chried it on. Thass all.

JOHN: I never.

JANE: You fuckin' did. You practically 'ad my bra off on top a' the bloody bus you did. Blimey.

JOHN: I –

TWIGS: An' on top a' that 'e on'y wears 'is fuckin' uniform don' 'e?

JOHN: So wot?

BILLY: ORDER!

JANE: OH FUCK OFF YOU! (*Moving away.*) Order this an' order that. Yore as bad as a fuckin' teacher yoo are. Woch yoo 'fink yoo are? Jus' 'cos yoo got a bleed'n gun. You can' even talk to a person wivout you wrap it up in a schoopid load a' rubbish I can' understand. I dunno oo you fink you are – soft in the 'ead you are if you want my opinion I tell you I don' care wot they done ter you or wot they done ter yore wife or to 'im neiver. It ain't my problem mate. I never done it. John never done it. Twigs never done it. We was in Woolies at the time. We was gettin' on wiv our lives which as it 'appens are quite complicated enough fankyou wiv John gettin' up my jersey all the time an' Twigs in a sulk an' not enough money fer decent cloves or goin' aht more than once in a blue moon blimey don' give me Asian this an' Asian that. I don' wanner know. I don't fuckin' care oo runs the counchry whevver iss the National Front or you lot or the p'lice force I don't care. So long as they leave me alone I don't care O.K? Mr. Cleverclogs. O.K?

BILLY: The witness is talking back. The witness refuses to be a witness. (*Almost with relief.*) Listen. How else do we make you see. How else are we going to get it through your heads eh? We speak. We march. We write. But we don't see it happening. You bring us up to believe in your way of change but I tell you we don't believe it any more. Out there will become a prison for us. And ignorance is no excuse.

JANE: YOU MAJ YORE POINT NOW LEAVE US ALONE!

BILLY: Ah. If it was as simple as that my dear we wouldn't be down here would we? We wouldn't be carrying these things. We would be somewhere safe and cosy I suppose while things went on pretty much as before. None of this would be happening. What is your name?

JANE: Jane Woods.

BILLY: Age?

JANE: Seventeen.

BILLY: Occupation?

JANE: Shop assistant.

BILLY: And where were you on October the 13th last?

JANE: I was – (*Pause.*) I was wiv 'im.

BILLY: You were with the accused.

JANE: We was tergevver.

BILLY: For how long?

JANE: Fer a week.

BILLY: This was a sexual liaison?

JANE: Oh it was. It def'nitely was. (*Aggressive.*) We stayed in a lit'l 'otel in Devon. An' we wen' aht every night. An' we went swimmin'. Wevver was great. An' we 'ad a fuckin' great bed. It was like an' 'oneymoon an' London an' coppers an' fights an' yoo lot you was nowhere O.K? There was just me an' 'im an' –

BILLY: Closing arguments.

JANE: I AIN'T FINISHED!

GANGE: Oh yes yoo fuckin' 'ave. 'Cos yoo may be pissed off wiv 'earin' abaht my problems gel but I'm well pissed off wiv people like you. I've 'ad enough a' this nuffink ter do wiv me crap. I've 'ad it. You got more than several racialist policemen on your schreets an' thass yore responsibility an' donch yoo give me no 'oneymoon crap!

BILLY: Arguments completed.

JANE: WELL ISN'T IT CHROO? DONCH YOO COME OVER 'ERE AN' TAKE OUR JOBS AN' WEAR FUNNY CLOVES AN' FUCK UP OUR LIVES AN' –

SAM: FOR GOD'S SAKE KEEP YOUR STUPID LITTLE TRAP SHUT GIRL!

BILLY: CLOSING ARGUMENTS COMPLETED!

SAM: THE MINUTE THEY HEAR THAT SHOT THEY'LL BE DOWN!

SMILER: PLEASE!

But BILLY *is moving towards* JOHN.

BILLY: We've tabled a list of perfectly reasonable demands. We've asked Mrs. Thatcher to crawl on her hands and knees down Whetstone High Street but they won't even send us one lousy S.P.G. officer –

Seizing JOHN *from behind and pinioning his arms.* GANGE *is holding up his gun.*

John Latham you have been found guilty of looking rather like an S.P.G. officer who wrongfully committed an accused on October the 13th last and as is the constituted authority of this court we will proceed to sentence which is that you will be taken from this place to this place which is a place of execution that is to say a courtroom that is to say a charnel house and that bullets will be fired into your body until you are dead.

GANGE *aiming at him.*

Fire. Fire. Fire. They won't send him. Fire.

GANGE: EVA-ANS! I WANT EV-ANS!

And, as if forced down out of his hand the gun points down to the floor.

BILLY: FIRE! FIRE! FIRE!

BILLY *is holding his pistol at JOHN's head and squeezes the trigger. Water pours out, drenching JOHN's hair and face as GANGE is shaking with internalised rage.*

GANGE: CANCH YOO UNDERSTAND A SIMPLE SENTENCE? (*Moving towards him across the floor.*) I wanted justice. I din' want no goon oo could 'ardly stand up. I want justice. I don't want questions in Parliament or smart answers. I want justice. I want that cunt oo sent me dahn. An' if you mus' know I ain't gonner put bullets inter ver bastard. I wanner give 'im some fist. Lots of it. Thass all.

BILLY: All talk.

GANGE: YORE ALL TALK! YORE THE ONE THASS ALL TALK! YOU WEREN' EVEN THERE WAS YOU? AN' AS FER YORE WIFE I NEVER SEEN YORE WIFE I DUNNO WHEVVER YOU 'AD A FUCKIN' WIFE! I WAS THERE SON NOT YOU! (*Right up to him.*) And lissen. If you wanner know it ain't as simple as you'd like it eiver. Not as simple an' not 'arf as complicated. If you reely wanner know I fuckin' did punch Evans, an' if there was competition as to oo could punch a paper bag or not well Evans wasn't it. I must a' bin the on'y geezer in the 'ole a' Souf'all oo was charged wiv 'ittin' ver right policeman. And *that* don't make no difference neiver. Becos I seen 'im 'ittin' kids oo *couldn't* punch a paper bag and that was good enough fer me. Justice is wot I seen on that occasion right? I ain't jreamin'. An' it ain't a mouf for an eye or wotevver neiver. Iss just that. Justice. Law a the fuckin' land. Punishment fer the crime. An' we ain't

got that 'ave we? (*Soft.*) An' I'll tell you one ovver fing. Look, when we go up against them we got ter go so fuckin' clean 'anded right? Becos they're chryin' all the time ter bend us. Ter bend us aht a shape. An' they bent you didn't they son? They bent you so far they bent you aht a shape. Well look. I ain't complainin'. But they ain't bent me. They never fuckin' will neiver an' when I go up against 'em I won't go wiv no rules an' no legal this and legal that an' no long words an' no clever-cunt schemes. I'll go real wild and as fer lightin' up the fuckin' sky oh you won't know it.

BILLY: NERVE! NERVE! IT'S YOU HASN'T GOT THE FUCKING NERVE!

GANGE *is at the door.*

GANGE: COME ON YOU CUNTS GIMME EVANS!

BILLY: PLE-EASE! PLE-EASE!

GANGE: EVANS EVANS COME ON GIMME EVANS YOU BASTARDS!

He has opened the door, is moving out . . .

CARM ON!

He's firing up into the stairwell, but he moves too far out. They must have marksmen up there and lots of them because the police bullets smash him back across the doorway tearing into him, ripping him back into the room. A horrible silence. Then a voice . . .

VOICE: I'm going to ask you to come out one by one.

Silence.

All of you to keep your hands up above your head. Well up above your head.

Silence.

Is that understood?

Silence.

There's no other way to leave.

BILLY: Well come on ladies and gentlemen! What do we have to be afraid of? They have laws out there.

Slowly JOHN starts to move towards the door. As he reaches it he puts his hands up.

I've heard your young girlfriend on the

subject. It's roses isn't it? Was it a honey-moon? Was that it? Don't delay. They ask you to crawl that's all. To raise your hands occasionally. On hands and knees. Obedience. That's all they want. A little obedience. The mountie's got his man. Fair cop.

And JOHN *goes.* JANE *is following, followed slowly by* TWIGS.

Step over him. *Step* over him. Haven't you heard our old Hindi proverb sahib. 'The way to prosperity is over the dead body of a friend.' Go on. You'll do fine. Out there it's all roses and champagne and honeymoons. My God the British Way of Life. I was raised on it sahib. You heard him on the subject. Didn't he hit the nail eh old bean? Go on. Go on. It's your bloody world sir.

SAM *and* SMILER *are left.* SMILER *starts to move towards the door.*

Listen you go on. Hands up. Show respect and fear. They like you to show fear. Oh he's right. That's your humble servant. Or was. Or was. Ah. But they haven't you know? They haven't bent me that far. Inside, inside myself they haven't you see – they haven't got to me. And it may be crazy but I carry it deep deep down in my heart and like him you see it is my law – me mine myself. This. (*Gestures at himself.*) Do you understand?

SMILER *has gone.* SAM *turns to him.*

SAM: Yes. Yes I do. (*Pause.*) You hold on to that.

And he's gone as well. BILLY *does a brief sketch of an Eastern obeisance but no more than a sketch. He stands quite still. Then he turns away from the door and* GANGE's *body and sits, cross-legged on the floor. With great calmness and dignity. A voice outside . . .*

VOICE: COME ON! YOU DEAF AND DUMB?

He continues to sit, quite impassively. Then again that voice, this time in danger of losing the easy dignity it has assumed during the proceedings.

I SAID COME ON! YOU DEAF AND DUMB YOU HALFWIT?

Still BILLY *sits. Then . . .*

I SAID ARE YOU DEAF AND DUMB

YOU PAKI HALFWIT!

BILLY: Deaf and dumb and bloody blind. (*Pause.*) Copper.

He sits impassively. Behind him in the doorway the dead boy. There are no more voices or interruptions and there is something about the way he holds himself that suggests that nothing will ever move him or change the blank patience on his face. Slow fade on BILLY *cross-legged centre-stage.*